CAMBRIDGE PRIMARY
Mathematics

Games Book

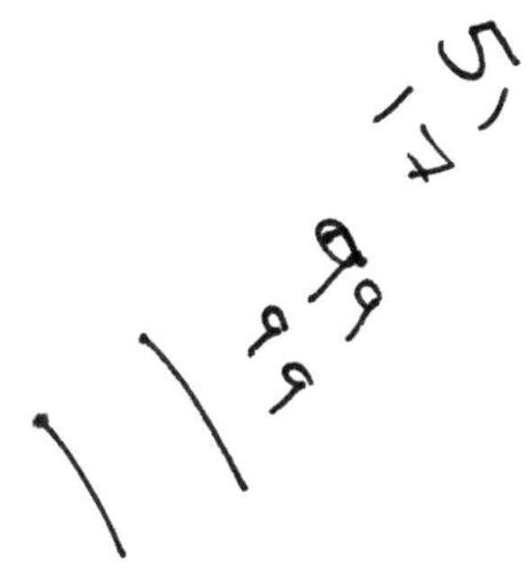

Cherri Moseley and Janet Rees

CAMBRIDGE
UNIVERSITY PRESS

University Printing House, Cambridge CB2 8BS, United Kingdom

One Liberty Plaza, 20th Floor, New York, NY 10006, USA

477 Williamstown Road, Port Melbourne, VIC 3207, Australia

4843/24, 2nd Floor, Ansari Road, Daryaganj, Delhi – 110002, India

79 Anson Road, #06–04/06, Singapore 079906

Cambridge University Press is part of the University of Cambridge.
It furthers the University's mission by disseminating knowledge in the pursuit of education, learning and research at the highest international levels of excellence.

Information on this title: education.cambridge.org

First published 2014
20 19 18 17 16 15 14 13 12

Printed in the United Kingdom by Latimer Trend

A catalogue record for this publication is available from the British Library

ISBN 978-1-107-69401-9 Paperback

Cover artwork: Bill Bolton

CD-ROM Terms and conditions of use

This End User License Agreement ('EULA') is a legal agreement between 'You' (which means the individual customer) and Cambridge University Press ('the Licensor') for *Cambridge Primary Mathematics Games Book Stage 3* CD-ROM ('the Product'). Please read this EULA carefully. By continuing to use the Product, You agree to the terms of this EULA. If You do not agree to this EULA, please do not use this Product and promptly return it to the place where you obtained it.

1. Licence
The Licensor grants You the right to use the Product under the terms of this EULA as follows:
(a) You may only install one copy of this Product (i) on a single computer or secure network server for use by one or more people at different times, or (ii) on one or more computers for use by a single person (provided the Product is only used on one computer at one time and is only used by that single person).
(b) You may only use the Product for non-profit, educational purposes.
(c) You shall not and shall not permit anyone else to: (i) copy or authorise copying of the Product, (ii) translate the Product, (iii) reverse-engineer, disassemble or decompile the Product, or (iv) transfer, sell, assign or otherwise convey any portion of the Product.

2. Copyright
(a) All content provided as part of the Product (including text, images and ancillary material) and all software, code, and metadata related to the Product is the copyright of the Licensor or has been licensed to the Licensor, and is protected by copyright and all other applicable intellectual property laws and international treaties.
(b) You may not copy the Product except for making one copy of the Product solely for backup or archival purposes. You may not alter, remove or destroy any copyright notice or other material placed on or with this Product.
(c) You may edit and make changes to any material provided in the Product in editable format ('Editable Material') and store copies of the resulting files ('Edited Files') for your own non-commercial, educational use, but You may not distribute Editable Materials or Edited Files to any third-party, or remove, alter, or destroy any copyright notices on Editable Materials or Edited Files, or copy any part of any Editable Material or Edited Files into any other file for any purpose whatsoever.

3. Liability and Indemnification
(a) The Product is supplied 'as-is' with no express guarantee as to its suitability. To the extent permitted by applicable law, the Licensor is not liable for costs of procurement of substitute products, damages or losses of any kind whatsoever resulting from the use of this Product, or errors or faults therein, and in every case the Licensor's liability shall be limited to the suggested list price or the amount actually paid by You for the Product, whichever is lower.
(b) You accept that the Licensor is not responsible for the persistency, accuracy or availability of any URLs of external or third-party internet websites referred to on the Product and does not guarantee that any content on such websites is, or will remain, accurate, appropriate or available. The Licensor shall not be liable for any content made available from any websites and URLs outside the Product or for the data collection or business practices of any third-party internet website or URL referenced by the Product.
(c) You agree to indemnify the Licensor and to keep indemnified the Licensor from and against any loss, cost, damage or expense (including without limitation damages paid to a third party and any reasonable legal costs) incurred by the Licensor as a result of your breach of any of the terms of this EULA.

4. Termination
Without prejudice to any other rights, the Licensor may terminate this EULA if You fail to comply with any of its terms and conditions. In such event, You must destroy all copies of the Product in your possession.

5. Governing law
This agreement is governed by the laws of England and Wales, without regard to its conflict of laws provision, and each party irrevocably submits to the exclusive jurisdiction of the English courts. The parties disclaim the application of the United Nations Convention on the International Sale of Goods.

Contents

Introduction

This Games Book consolidates and reinforces mathematical learning for Stage 3 learners (usually 7–8 years). It can be used as an independent resource for anyone wanting to encourage mathematical learning in children, or as a supplementary part of the *Cambridge Primary Mathematics* series.

If used as part of the series alongside the *Teacher's Resource 3* (9781107668898), then you will often be going directly to a specific game and page number according to the reference in the '*More activities*' section in the *Teacher's Resource* and will therefore already be familiar with the learning outcome of the game. If you are using the book as an independent resource, you can use the Objective map on the CD-ROM to help you determine what game you might want to play according to what learning outcome you are after, or you can simply read the '*Maths focus*' at the start of each game to decide if it's appropriate.

The games are grouped by strand, i.e. 'Number', 'Geometry', 'Measure' and 'Handling data' so that an independent user can easily navigate the pool of games. For those of you using this book alongside the *Teacher's Resource 3*, you will find that the games within a strand are ordered according to the order in which they are referenced in the *Teacher's Resource 3* (if you grouped all chapters of a given strand together).

Please note that the *Games Book* on its own does **not** cover all of the Cambridge Primary mathematics curriculum framework for Stage 3.

All games boards, game cards and record sheets provided within the printed book are also available on the CD-ROM for quick printing if preferred. Some games boards and resources will also be provided as Word documents so that you can adapt them as required. The CD-ROM also provides child-friendly instructions for each game, which can be displayed at the front of the class or sent home with the games for independent play. Nets for making dice, spinners and other useful mathematical resources are also provided as printable PDFs on the CD-ROM.

This publication is part of the *Cambridge Primary Maths* project. *Cambridge Primary Maths* is an innovative combination of curriculum and resources designed to support teachers and learners to succeed in primary mathematics through best-practice international maths teaching and a problem-solving approach.

Cambridge Primary Maths brings together the world-class Cambridge Primary mathematics curriculum from Cambridge International Examinations, high-quality publishing from Cambridge University Press and expertise in engaging online enrichment materials for the mathematics curriculum from NRICH.

Teachers have access to an online tool that maps resources and links to materials offered through the primary mathematics curriculum, NRICH and Cambridge Primary mathematics textbooks and e-books. These resources include engaging online activities, best-practice guidance and examples of *Cambridge Primary Maths* in action.

The Cambridge curriculum is dedicated to helping schools develop learners who are confident, responsible, reflective, innovative and engaged. It is designed to give learners the skills to problem solve effectively, apply mathematical knowledge and develop a holistic understanding of the subject.

The *Cambridge Primary Maths* textbooks provide best-in-class support for this problem-solving approach, based on pedagogical practice found in successful schools across the world. The engaging NRICH online resources help develop mathematical thinking and problem-solving skills. To get involved visit www.cie.org.uk/cambridgeprimarymaths

The benefits of being part of *Cambridge Primary Maths* are:

- the opportunity to explore a maths curriculum founded on the values of the University of Cambridge and best practice in schools
- access to an innovative package of online and print resources that can help bring the Cambridge Primary mathematics curriculum to life in the classroom.

This series is arranged to ensure that the curriculum is covered whilst allowing teachers to use a flexible approach. The Scheme of Work for Stage 3 has been followed, though not in the same order and there will be some deviations. The components are:

- Teacher's Resource 3 ISBN: 9781107668898 (printed book and CD-ROM).
- Learner's Book 3 ISBN: 9781107667679 (printed book)
- Games Book 3 ISBN: 9781107694019 (printed book and CD-ROM).

For associated NRICH activities, please visit the *Cambridge Primary Maths* project at www.cie.org.uk/cambridgeprimarymaths

Place value games 3Np.01

Largest and smallest

Maths focus: To understand what each digit represents in three-digit numbers.

A game for six players.

What you need:
- Place value cards (CD-ROM).

Instructions

1 Shuffle a set of hundreds, tens and ones place value cards.
2 Place the three piles face down on the table.
3 Call out the names of six players: two of them take a card from the top of each pile. The six players quickly confer to make the largest and smallest numbers, showing the class the three-digit numbers.
4 The class checks that they have made the largest and smallest numbers with those place value cards. Repeat with another six learners.

Three counts 3Nc.02

Maths focus: Counting on in ones, tens or hundreds from any number.

A game for the whole class.

Instructions

1 Split the class into three groups: the ones, the tens and the hundreds.
2 Call out a start number and point to one of the groups.
3 This group must count on from the start number according to their group. So if you start at 124 and point to the tens group, they should say, "134, 144, 154, 164, 174".
4 Point to the hundreds group so that they take over the count ("274, 374, 484..."). Vary by telling groups to count backwards.

Pair counting 3Nc.02

Maths focus: Counting on in ones, tens or hundreds from any number.

A game for two players.

What you need:
- Small ball or bean bag.

Instructions

1 Put the players in pairs facing each other and give each pair a ball or bean bag.
2 Call out a start number, the step size (1, 10 or 100) and either 'forward' or 'back'.
3 Players say the next number as they throw the ball to and from each other.
4 Call out a stop number or change the count.

Three rings

Maths focus: To understand what each digit represents in three-digit numbers.

A game for two to four players.

What you need:
- Three hoops and seven bean bags.

Instructions

1 Place three hoops on the floor, one represents hundreds, one represents tens and one represents ones.

2 Give player's seven bean bags or stones to throw into the hoops.

3 How many different three-digit numbers can they make?

On the Line

Maths focus: Read numbers to 999, understanding what each digit represents by partitioning into hundreds, tens and units; place a three-digit number on a number line marked off in multiples of 10.

A game for two players.

What you need:
- The On the line board (p3).
- One or two dice (alternatively, a 1 to 9 spinner or a set of Hundreds and tens place value cards (CD-ROM)).
- Two different coloured pencils.
- Scissors.
- Adhesive tape.

Using scissors and adhesive tape, construct the On the line game board.

Instructions

1 Players take it in turn to roll the two dice (or roll the same dice twice) to create a three-digit multiple of 10.

2 The first number rolled is the hundreds, the second is the tens. So 4, then 6 would make 460. (Alternatively, players could spin the spinner twice or select one hundreds and one tens place value card from a jumbled set face down on the table.)

3 Players then mark their number on the number line in their chosen colour.

4 The winner is the first player to mark three numbers in a row on the number line, without a number from the other player in between.

For a more strategic game, a player can choose which of the two numbers they generate is the hundreds and which number is the tens.

For a more challenging game, use a number line marked in hundreds only. They could also generate three digits rather than two.

On the line

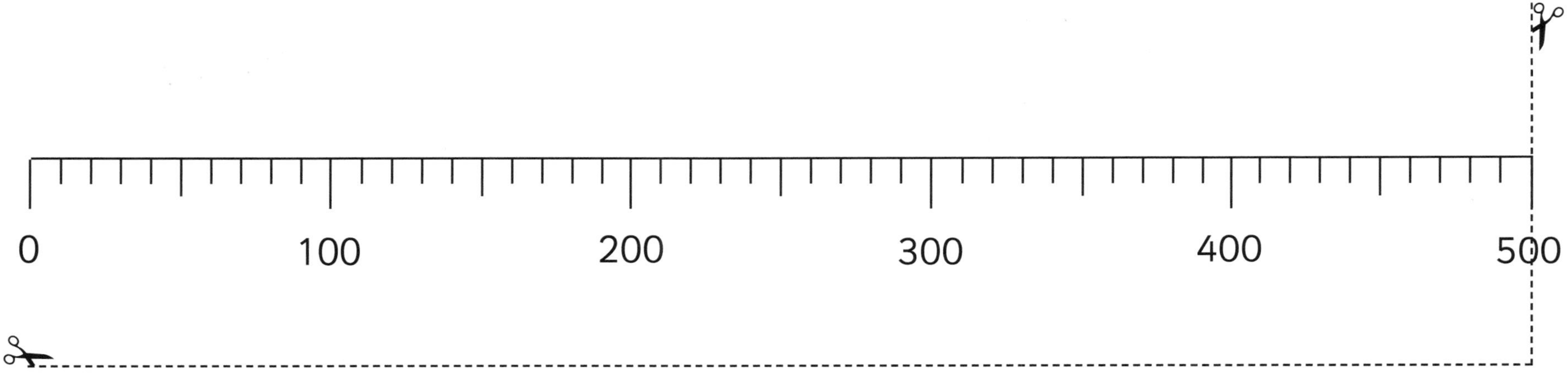

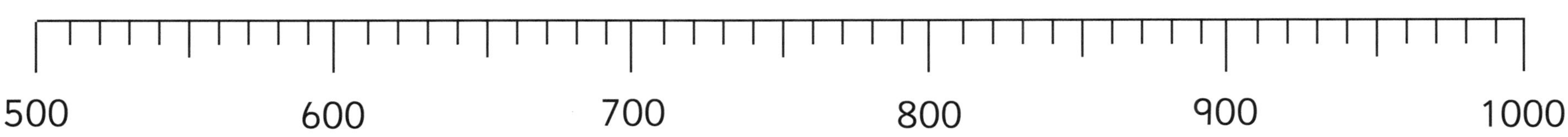

Addition game

Maths focus: Adding several small numbers and adding two-digit numbers, reordering as they choose, to assist the calculation.

A game for two players.

What you need:

- Game board 1 (p5) or Game board 2 (p6).
- A 1–10 spinner (CD-ROM).

Instructions

1 Each player takes it in turn to spin the spinner.

2 Players write the number generated in their grid twice (they can write the number in any square, but the squares must not be next to each other – in the same row or column or diagonal).

3 Once the grid is filled, each player adds each row and column, entering the totals in the right hand column and bottom row.

4 Players then add the totals in the final row and column to reach a final total. The player with the highest total is the winner.

Two versions of the game are provided, Game 1 has fewer squares to fill and consequently fewer additions to make.

Game 1 could have the first row and column blanked out so there are only three numbers to add.

Double and half pelmanism

Maths focus: By finding pairs of numbers which are the double and half of each other, learners recognise the relationship between doubling and halving.

A game for two players.

What you need:

- Double and half pelmanism cards (pp7–8).
- Thin card.
- Scissors.

Instructions

1 Shuffle the cards and lay them out face down in a 6 by 5 grid.

2 Players take it in turn to turn over any two cards.

3 If the cards show two numbers which are the double and half of each other (for example 2 and 4 or 25 and 50), the player keeps the cards. Cards which do not match are returned face down in the same position.

4 The winner is the player with the most cards when all pairs have been matched and collected.

Addition game 1

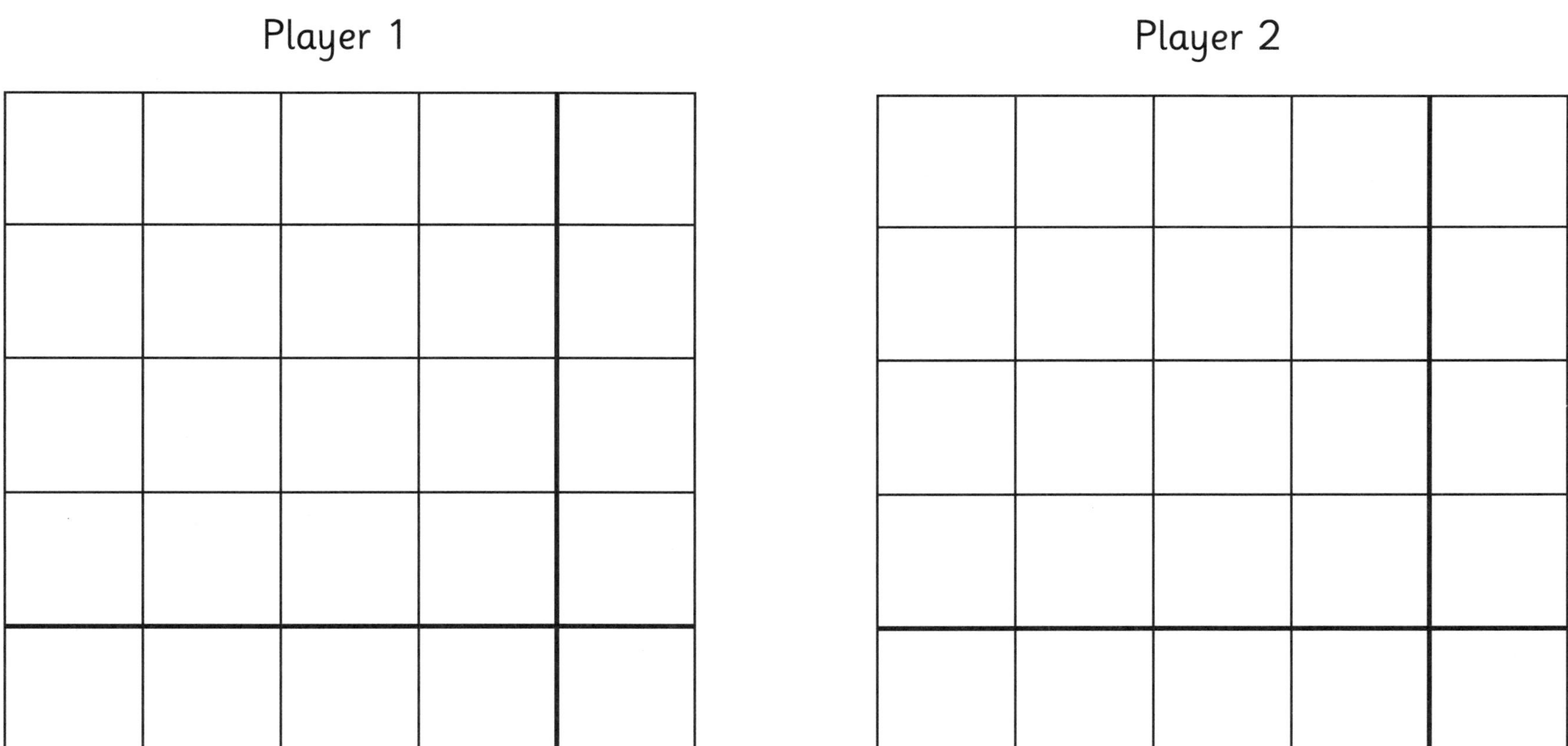

Addition game 2

Player 1

Player 2

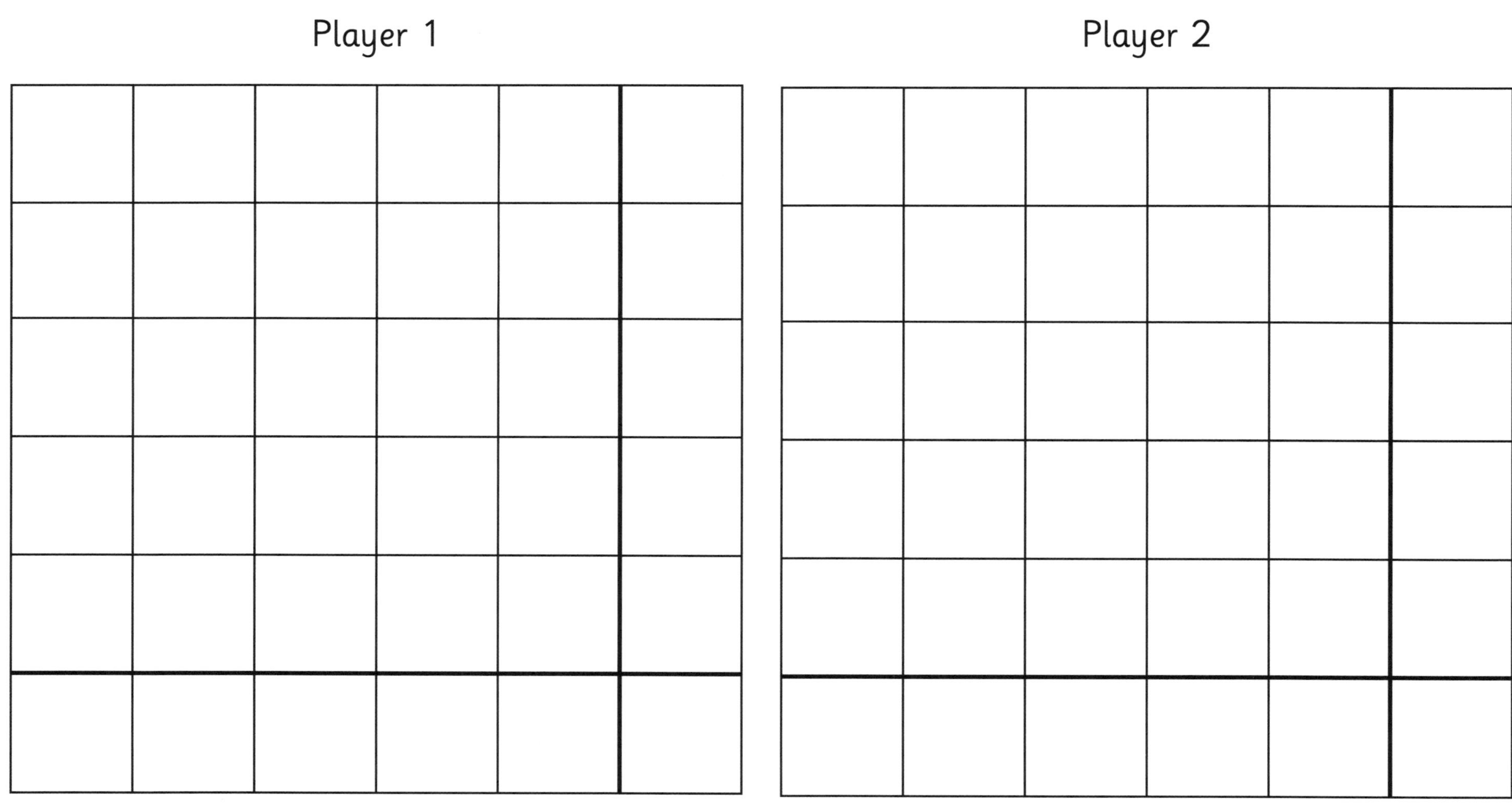

Double and half pelmanism – cards

2	3	4
5	6	7
9	10	11
13	14	15
16	17	18

19	22	25
26	30	32
34	35	38
40	45	50
70	80	90

Target dice

3Ni.02

Maths focus: Adding and subtracting three or more small numbers to reach a target number.

A game for two players.

What you need:

- A set of 0–9 digit cards (CD-ROM).
- Three dice.
- Counters.

Instructions

1 Shuffle the cards and put them in a pile face down.

2 Players take it in turn to turn over the top card. This is the target number.

3 Players take it turns to roll the dice. At each roll of the dice, both players are looking for the target number. They can add or subtract the numbers on the dice but must use all three numbers.

4 The first player to call out the target number wins a counter. A player can make a challenge if they cannot see how the total was made. If their challenge is correct, they take a counter from the other player.

5 After a few turns, turn over the top card to get a new target number.

6 The winner is the first player to collect 10 counters.

For a more challenging game: use four or five dice. Alternatively, use different dice (for example 7 to 12) and a larger number of target cards.

The multiples game

3Ni.07

Maths focus: Recognising multiples of 2, 3, 4 and 5 to 50.

A game for two or three players.

What you need:

- The multiples game board (p10).
- A 1–6 dice (CD-ROM).
- Counters in three different colours.
- 100 square (CD-ROM).

Instructions

1 Players take it in turns to roll the dice. If the dice shows 1 or 6, they miss a turn; if the dice shows 2, 3, 4 or 5 they must say a multiple of that number and place one of their counters on that number.

2 Players can challenge each other if they do not think the number named is a multiple of the number on the dice. If the challenger is correct, the player cannot put a counter on the number they claimed during that turn.

3 Players aim to make sticks (across) or towers (up or down) of four counters in a row (or column) on the board.

The winner is the player with the highest number of sticks and towers when all the multiples of 2, 3, 4 and 5 have been claimed.

For a more challenging game, use a 100 square as the board. The winner could be the first player to get five sticks (across) or towers (up or down) of four counters in a row (or column) on the board.

Alternatively, the players could agree a target number of sticks and towers or change the length of the sticks and towers.

The multiples game

1	2	3	4	5	6	7	8	9	10
11	12	13	14	15	16	17	18	19	20
21	22	23	24	25	26	27	28	29	30
31	32	33	34	35	36	37	38	39	40
41	42	43	44	45	46	47	48	49	50

Domino multiplication

Maths focus: Multiplying by 0, 1, 2, 3, 4 and 5 and adding the totals.

A game for two or three players.

What you need:

- A set of double 6 dominoes (CD-ROM).
- Paper and pencil.

Instructions

1. Remove any domino with a six on it from the set.
2. Turn the rest of the dominoes face down and mix them up.
3. Players take it in turns to take a domino and turn it face up. They multiply the two numbers shown together to get their score (so if 2 and 5 are shown, the score is 2×5 or 5×2, which equals 10).
4. The domino is then discarded.
5. Players keep a running total of their score.
6. The player with the highest score when all the dominos have been used is the winner.

Adding 10 and 100 game

Maths focus: Find 10 and 100 more than two- and three-digit numbers.

A game for 2 to 4 players.

What you need:

- The 10 and 100 game board (p13).
- A different coloured counter for each player.
- A 1–6 dice (CD-ROM).
- Optional – a set of Place value cards (CD-ROM), excluding the single digits.

Instructions

Each player begins with a score of 10.

1. Players take it in turns to roll the dice and move their counter accordingly on the game board.
2. Players land on a 0, 10 or 100 and add that number to their score.
3. The game ends when all the players have landed on 'Finish'.
4. The winner is the player with the highest final score.

Players could also mark their score on a 0 to 1000 number line (marked either in tens or hundreds).

Some players may find Place value cards useful to help with adding on 10 or 100.

For a more challenging game: ask players to start with a score of any single digit number.

Subtracting 10 and 100 game

Maths focus: Find 10 and 100 less than two- and three-digit numbers.

3Nc.02

A game for 2 to 4 players.

What you need:
- The 10 and 100 game board (p13).
- A different coloured counter for each player.
- A 1–6 dice (CD-ROM).
- Optional – a set of Place value cards (CD-ROM), excluding the single digits.

Instructions

Each player begins with a score of 1000.

1 Players take it in turns to roll a dice and move their counter accordingly on the game board.

2 Players land on a 0, 10 or 100 and subtract that number from their score.

3 The game ends when all the players have landed on 'Finish'.

4 The winner is the player with the lowest final score.

Some players may find Place value cards useful to help with adding on 10 or 100.

Players could also mark their score on a 0 to 1000 number line (marked either in tens or hundreds).

For a more challenging game: ask players to start with a score of 99? (where ? is any single digit number).

Greater than or less than?

Maths focus: Quick recognition of a three-digit number and comparison with another number, before recognising which is greater.

A game for two players.

What you need:
- The Greater than or less than (p14) sheet printed on thin card.
- Scissors.

Instructions

1 Cut out the number cards.

2 Place them face down on the table and mix them up.

3 Both players pick up a card and turn it over at the same time.

4 They both look at the numbers.

5 The player whose number is greater says:

6 '_____ is greater than _____'.

7 The player whose number is less says:

8 '_____ is less than _____'.

9 The player who speaks first claims both number cards.

10 The winner is the player who collects the most cards.

10 and 100 game

Start	0	0	10	0	0	10	0
							100
0	0	10	100	0	10	0	0
100							
0	10	0	10	0	10	0	0
							100
0	0	10	0	10	0	10	0
100							
0	10	0	10	100	0	10	0
							100
0	10	0	100	0	10	0	10
100							
0	0	10	10	10	0	10	Finish

Greater than or less than?

167	671	716	617
246	264	426	462
468	486	684	648
864	846	624	642
176	761	359	394
594	549	935	953
872	827	278	287
728	782	876	678

Ranges

Maths focus: Estimating the total of four numbers and checking the total against a range.

A game for two players.

What you need:

- A set of Number cards (CD-ROM), 10 to 50.
- Paper and pencil.
- Some counters.
- A calculator (optional).

Instructions

1 Shuffle the cards well and place them face down on the table.
2 Players take it in turns to turn over the top four cards and place them in front of themselves.
3 The player quickly estimates the total.
4 The players then add the numbers in any way they choose to see how close the player was. (Each player has a range of 10, five less than the actual total and five more than the actual total. So if the player estimates 65, their range is 60 to 70.)
5 If the total is within the range, the player can claim a counter.
6 The player with the most counters after five turns each is the winner.

It may be necessary to quickly cover the cards so that the player cannot work out the total before they say their estimate.

For a more challenging game: extend the number and range of cards.

For an easier game: extend the range to 20, 10 less than the actual total and 10 more than the actual total.

The add and subtract game

Maths focus: Adding and subtracting to find a particular total.

A game for two players.

What you need:

- The Add and Subtract game board (pp16–17) (either board 1 or 2, or both boards).
- Two dice (CD-ROM).
- Paper and pencil.
- Counters in two different colours.
- A calculator (optional).

Instructions

Playing with one board:

Players take it in turns to roll the dice.

1 The first player rolls both dice and uses the numbers shown to create a two-digit number.
2 The player then tries to find a calculation on the board which has that number as the answer, and, if successful, puts one of their counters on it.
3 If no calculation has that answer, they miss that turn.
4 The winner is the player with the most counters on the board.

Playing with both boards:

As above but the players have a board each. The winner is the player with the most counters on their board after an agreed length of time.

The add and subtract game: board 1

60 − 9	13 + 10	45 − 13	31 + 32
7 + 8	66 − 12	27 + 9	50 − 6
40 + 15	15 + 16	21 + 21	22 − 6

The add and subtract game: board 2

11 + 11	50 − 7	22 + 23	75 + 13
60 − 4	14 + 10	50 − 9	6 + 7
26 + 26	20 − 8	52 − 18	17 + 18

Making tens

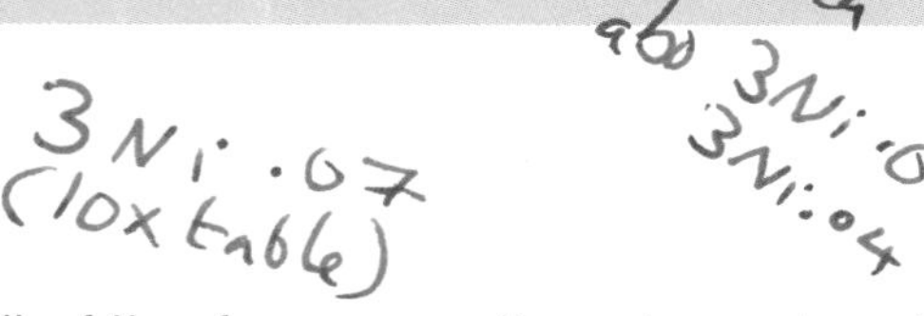

Maths focus: Use any or all of the four operations to make a multiple of 10.

A game for two to six players.

What you need:
- A set of double six dominoes (CD-ROM).
- Paper and pencil.

Instructions

The aim of the game is to make a multiple of 10 using any two of the three dominoes selected each turn.

Numbers can be added, subtracted, multiplied or divided in any way the player chooses – so if the dominoes turned over were:

2|3; 5|1 and 4|2, they could say

$1 \times 5 = 5$, $2 + 3 = 5$, so 5 and 5 is 10.

Score one point for one ten.

Alternatively, they could say:

$4 + 2 = 6$, $5 \times 1 = 5$, $5 \times 6 = 30$

and score three points for three tens.

Place a set of dominoes face down on the table and mix them up.

1 Players take it in turns to take three dominoes and place them face up on the table.
2 Players decide which calculations to make with the two dominoes selected from the three taken. Players keep the dominoes used to make tens to one side. These dominoes are no longer in play. During their next turn, players pick two more dominoes to go with the unused domino.
3 If a player cannot make a multiple of 10, their score for that round is zero and they return all three dominoes to the rest of the pile.
4 At the end of five rounds, the winner is the player with the most points.

Multiple mayhem

Maths focus: Multiplying single digit numbers by 2, 3, 4, 5, 9 and 10.

A game for two or three players.

What you need:
- The Multiple mayhem game board (p19).
- Two 1–6 dice (CD-ROM) with the 'ones' changed to 'tens' on each dice and one of the 'sixes' changed to a 'nine'.
- A different coloured counter for each player.

Instructions

Players take it in turns to roll both dice.

1 One player rolls both dice and multiplies the two numbers shown on their dice together, in any order they choose, to find the number of spaces to move on the game board. (If 2 and 9 are thrown, the calculation: $2 \times 9 = 18$ is made, the player counts on 18 from where they were.)
2 If they go beyond 100, players continue counting from 1. So if they are on 84 and roll 2×10, the player's counter would be placed on 4.
3 The first player to land on 100 is the winner.

Multiple mayhem

1	2	3	4	5	6	7	8	9	10
11	12	13	14	15	16	17	18	19	20
21	22	23	24	25	26	27	28	29	30
31	32	33	34	35	36	37	38	39	40
41	42	43	44	45	46	47	48	49	50
51	52	53	54	55	56	57	58	59	60
61	62	63	64	65	66	67	68	69	70
71	72	73	74	75	76	77	78	79	80
81	82	83	84	85	86	87	88	89	90
91	92	93	94	95	96	97	98	99	100

All round

Maths focus: Rounding to the nearest 10 or 100.

A game for two players.

What you need:

- A copy of the All Round game board, either Rounding Board 1 (p21) or Rounding Board 2 (p22).
- A 0 to 9 spinner (CD-ROM).
- Counters in two different colours.

Instructions: Rounding to the nearest 10

Use Rounding Board 1.

1 Players take it in turns to spin the spinner twice to create a two-digit number. If the first digit is zero, players will be creating a single digit number.

2 They round the number to the nearest 10 and place a counter on that tens number.

3 The winner is the first player to have one of their counters on every number.

Instructions: Rounding to the nearest 100

Use Rounding Board 2.

1 Players take it in turns to spin the spinner three times to create a three-digit number. If the first digit is zero, players will be creating a two digit number.

2 They round the number to the nearest 100 and place a counter on that hundreds number.

3 The winner is the first player to have one of their counters on every number.

Numbers could also be generated with Place Value (CD-ROM) or Digit Cards (CD-ROM) or with cloakroom tickets.

All round

Rounding Board 1	0	10
20	30	40
50	60	70
80	90	100

All round

Rounding Board 2	0	100
200	300	400
500	600	700
800	900	1000

Collect a fraction 1

Maths focus: Recognise that two quarters are equivalent to one half and recognise mixed numbers.

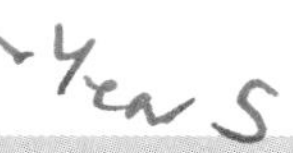

A game for two to four players.

What you need:

- Several copies of Halves and Quarters circles (p24).
- A 1–6 dice (CD-ROM) or blank spinner labelled $\frac{1}{4}$, $\frac{1}{4}$, $\frac{1}{2}$, $\frac{1}{2}$, 0, 0 (CD-ROM).
- Scissors.
- Coloured paper (optional).

Instructions

1. Print or copy and cut out several copies of the Halves and quarters sheet. Ideally, the halves should be one colour and the quarters another.
2. Prepare the dice by putting a sticker over the existing numbers and writing the above numbers on it. Alternatively, print out the six-section spinner and write the above numbers on it.
3. Players take it in turns to roll the dice and collect the number of halves or quarters shown.
4. As the players collect their fractions, they complete as many circles as they can.
5. After five turns each, players identify their total number of circles and record this as a mixed number, for example, $4\frac{1}{4}$.
6. The winner is the player who has collected the most circles. A number line marked in quarters could be used to compare and check numbers.

Collect a fraction 2

Maths focus: Recognise equivalent and simple mixed fractions.

A game for two to four players.

What you need:

- A 1–6 dice (CD-ROM) or blank spinner labelled $\frac{1}{4}$, $\frac{1}{2}$, $\frac{1}{3}$, $\frac{1}{8}$, $\frac{1}{10}$ and 0 (CD-ROM).
- Several copies of all the fraction circles: Halves and Quarters (p24), Thirds and eighths (p25) and Tenths (p26).
- Scissors.
- Coloured paper (optional).

Instructions

1. Print or copy and cut out several copies of each circle. Ideally, each type of fraction should be on different coloured paper.
2. Prepare the dice by putting a sticker over the existing numbers and writing the above numbers on it. Alternatively, print out the six-section spinner and write the above numbers on it.
3. Players take it in turns to roll the dice and collect the fraction shown.
4. As the players collect their fractions, they complete as many circles as they can. Complete circles can be made from different fractions.
5. After five turns each, players record the total of their collected fractions as a mixed number, for example, $4\frac{1}{4}$. Players may swap pieces for equivalent fraction to help find their total.
6. The winner is the player who has collected the most circles.

Halves and quarters

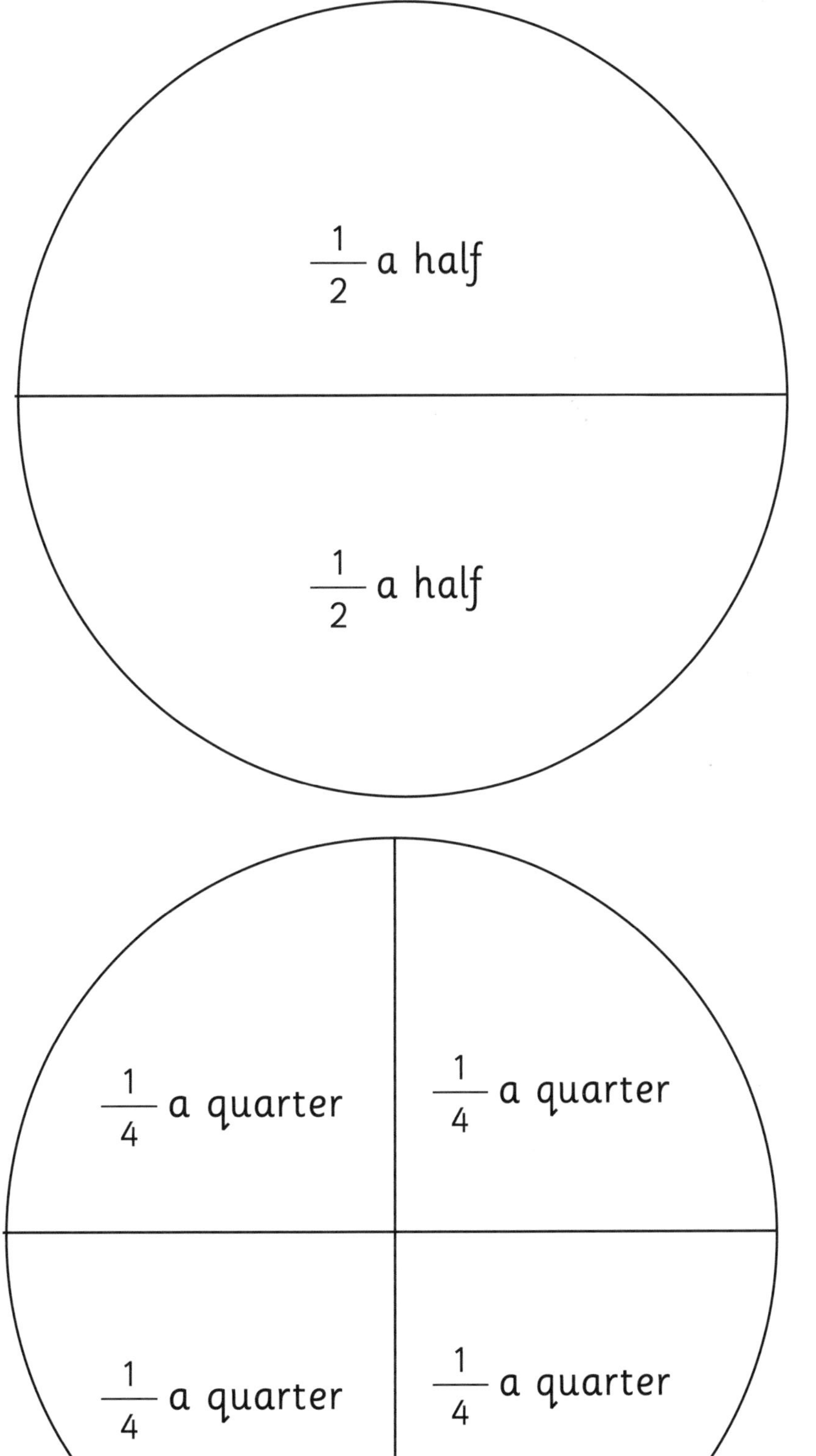

Thirds and eighths

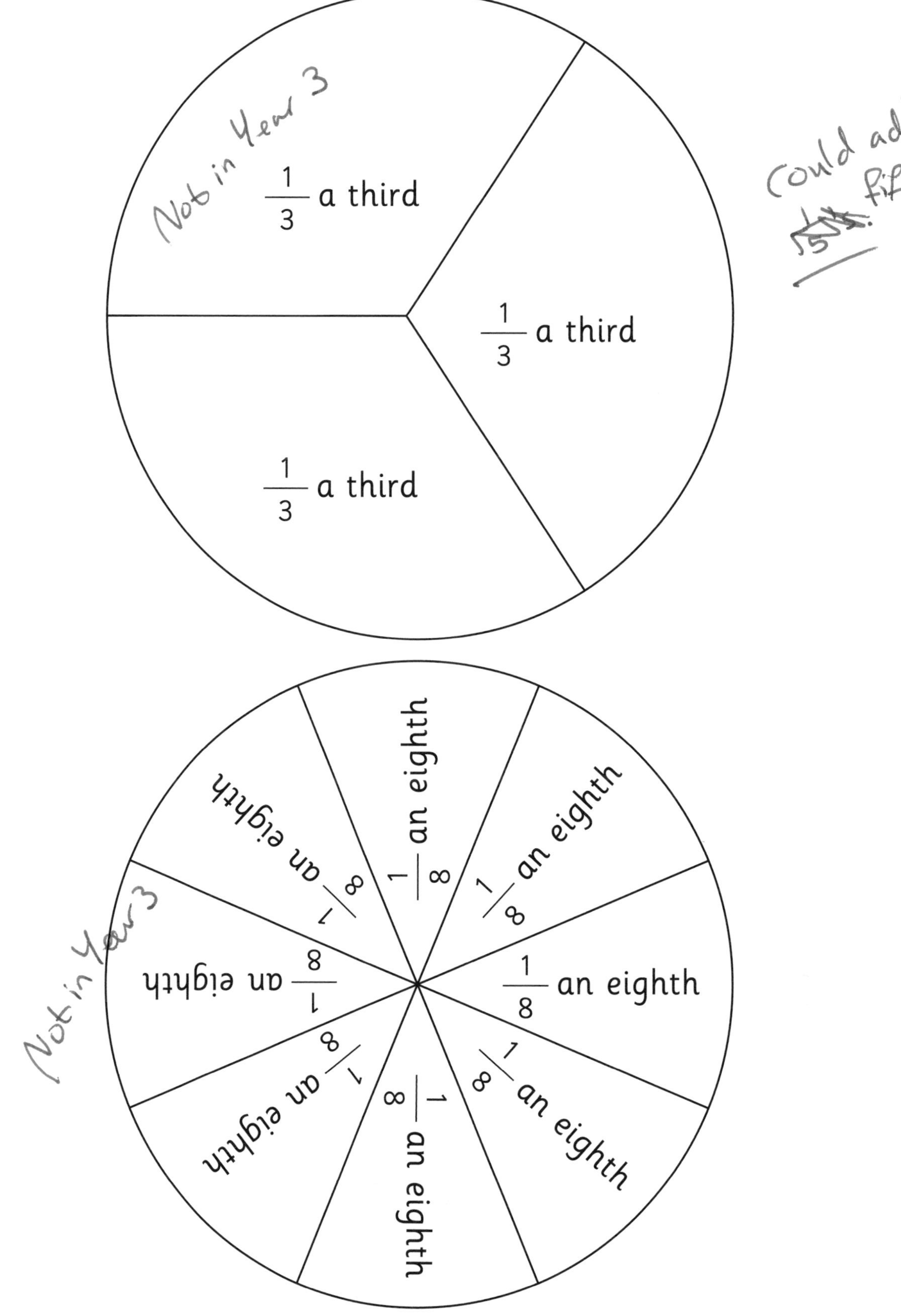

Tenths

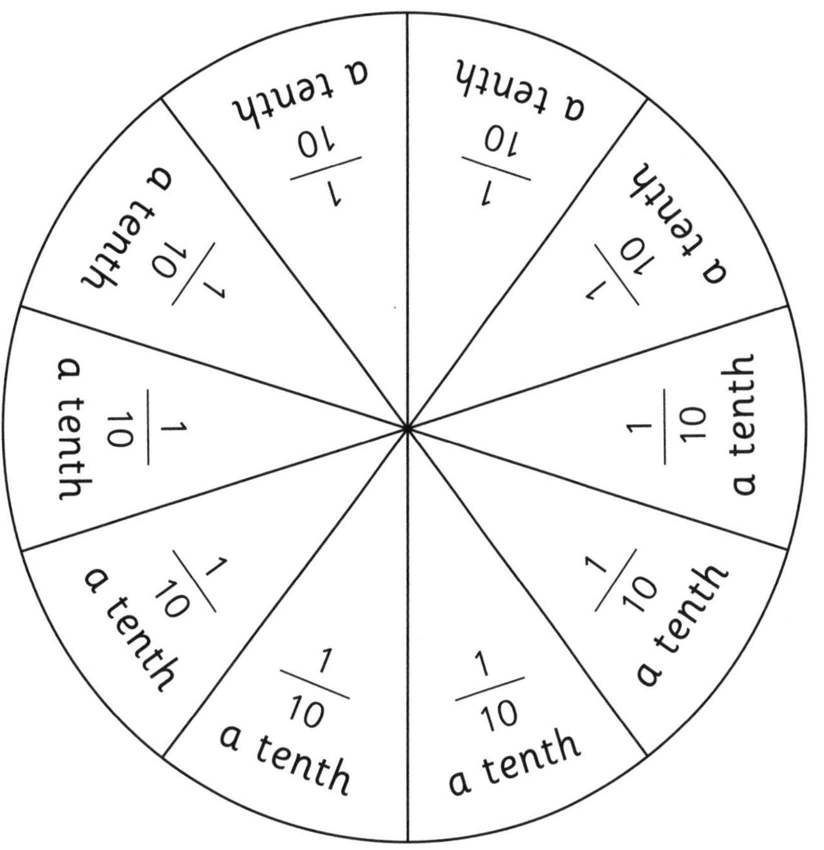

1/10
a tenth
1/10
a tenth
1/10
a tenth
1/10
a tenth
1/10
a tenth
1/10
a tenth
1/10
a tenth
1/10
a tenth
1/10
a tenth
1/10
a tenth

Halves game

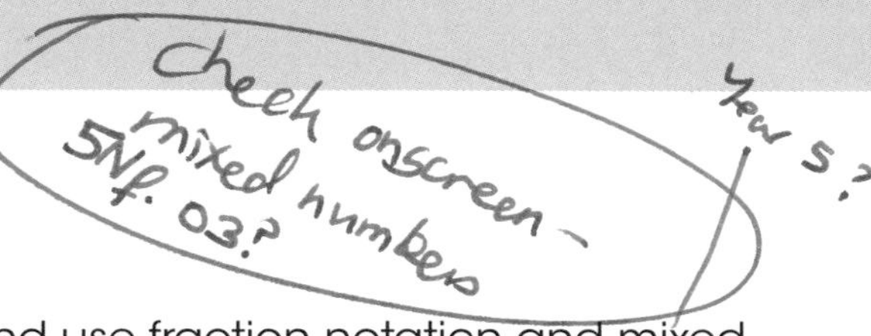

Maths focus: Recognise and use fraction notation and mixed numbers and understand that two quarters are equivalent to one half.

A game for two to four players.

What you need:
- The Halves Game board (p28).
- A Halves game 0–10 number line (p29) for each player.
- A different coloured counter for each player.
- A 1–6 dice (CD-ROM).

Instructions

1 Players take it in turns to roll a dice and move their counter accordingly.

2 When they land on a square with a semi-circle in it, they draw a jump of $\frac{1}{2}$ on their number line. For example, for the first semi-circle, they draw a jump from 0 to $\frac{1}{2}$, and circle the $\frac{1}{2}$ on the number line. Their number line shows how many semi-circles they have collected, which is their current score.

3 The winner is the player with the highest score once everyone has landed on finish.

For a more complex game, add some pictures of quarter circles to the game board. Players mark the halves and quarters on their number line in the same way to identify their score. Some learners may need support to add $\frac{1}{2}$ to scores such as $1\frac{3}{4}$, or $2\frac{1}{4}$.

Quarters game

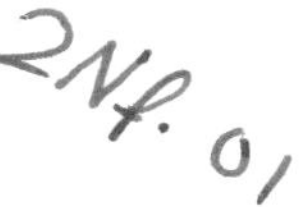

Maths focus: Recognise a quarter and three-quarters of a shape and that two quarters are equivalent to one half.

A game for two to four players.

What you need:
- A copy of the Quarters game board (p30) for each player.
- A dice or spinner (CD-ROM).
- Sticky labels.
- Colouring pencils.

Instructions

Prepare the dice by putting a sticky label over the existing numbers and writing a fraction: $\frac{1}{4}$, $\frac{1}{4}$, $\frac{2}{4}$, $\frac{1}{2}$, $\frac{3}{4}$, $\frac{3}{4}$ on each face. Alternatively, make a six-section spinner and write the fractions given above on each section.

1 Players take it in turns to roll the dice or spin the spinner and colour the fraction shown on one of their shapes.

2 The winner is the first player to have coloured all of their shapes.

For a slightly different game, allow the players to split the fraction rolled so that they can colour the matching amount over two or three shapes.

Halves Game

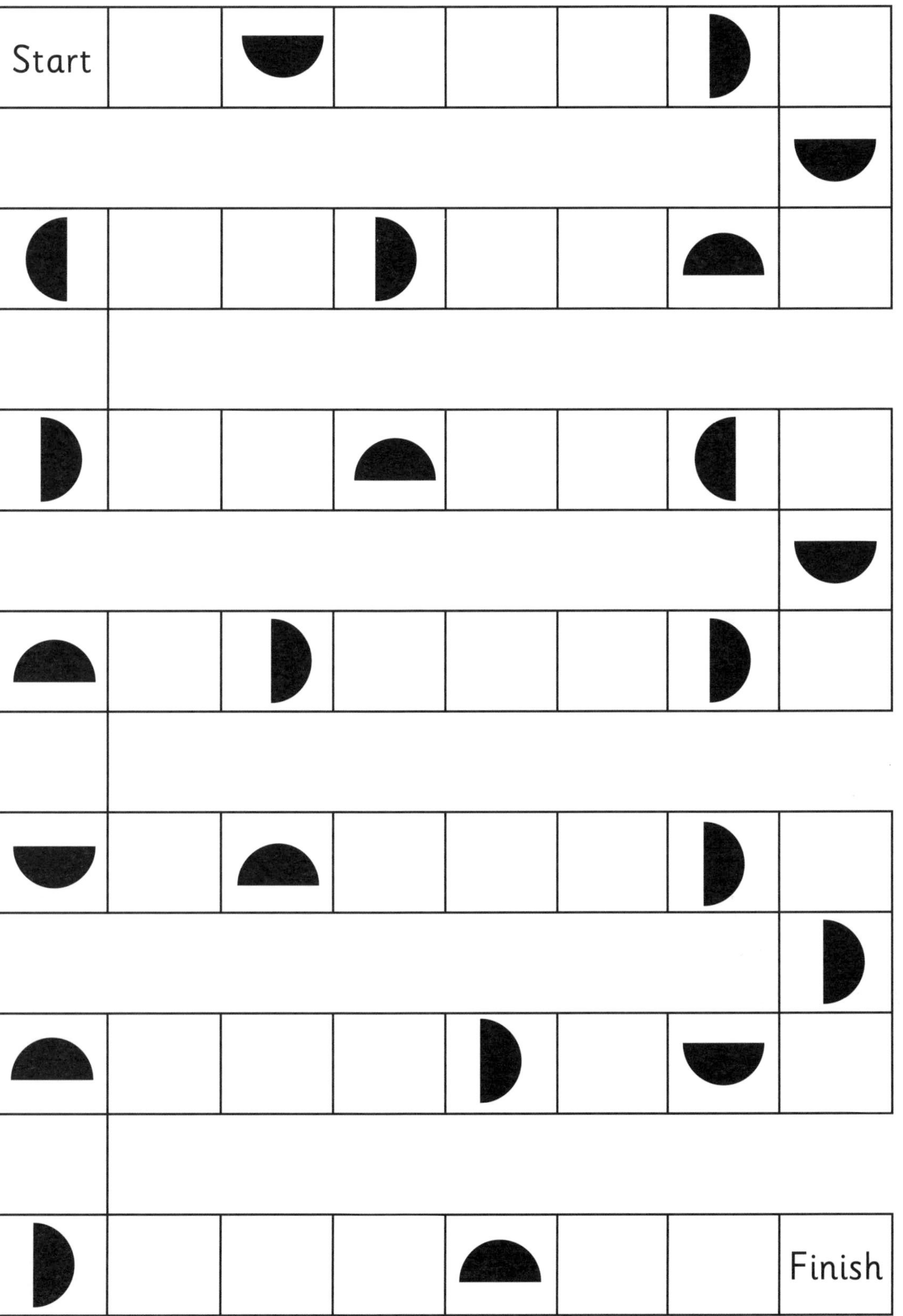

Halves game 0–10 Number line

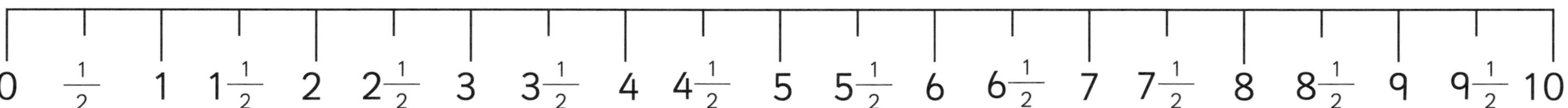

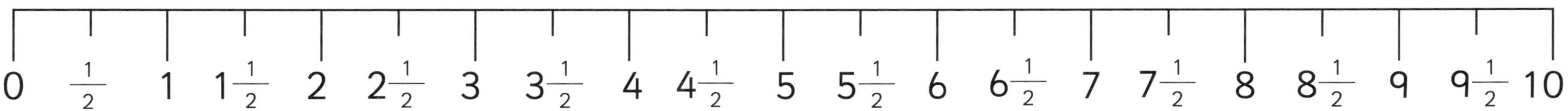

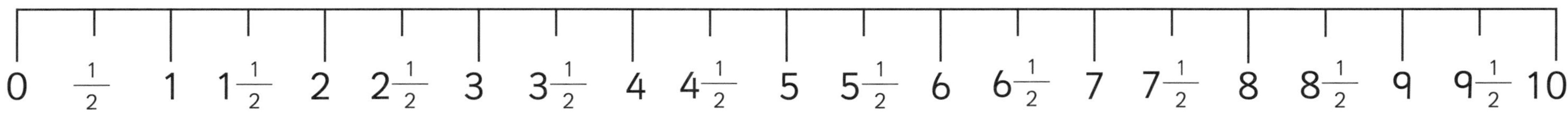

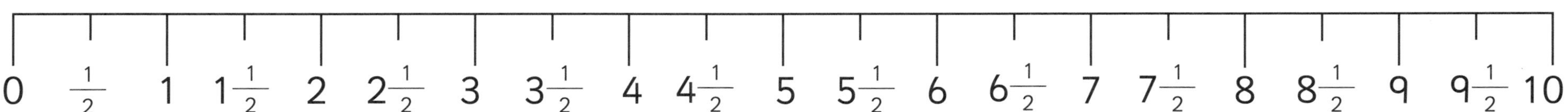

Quarters game

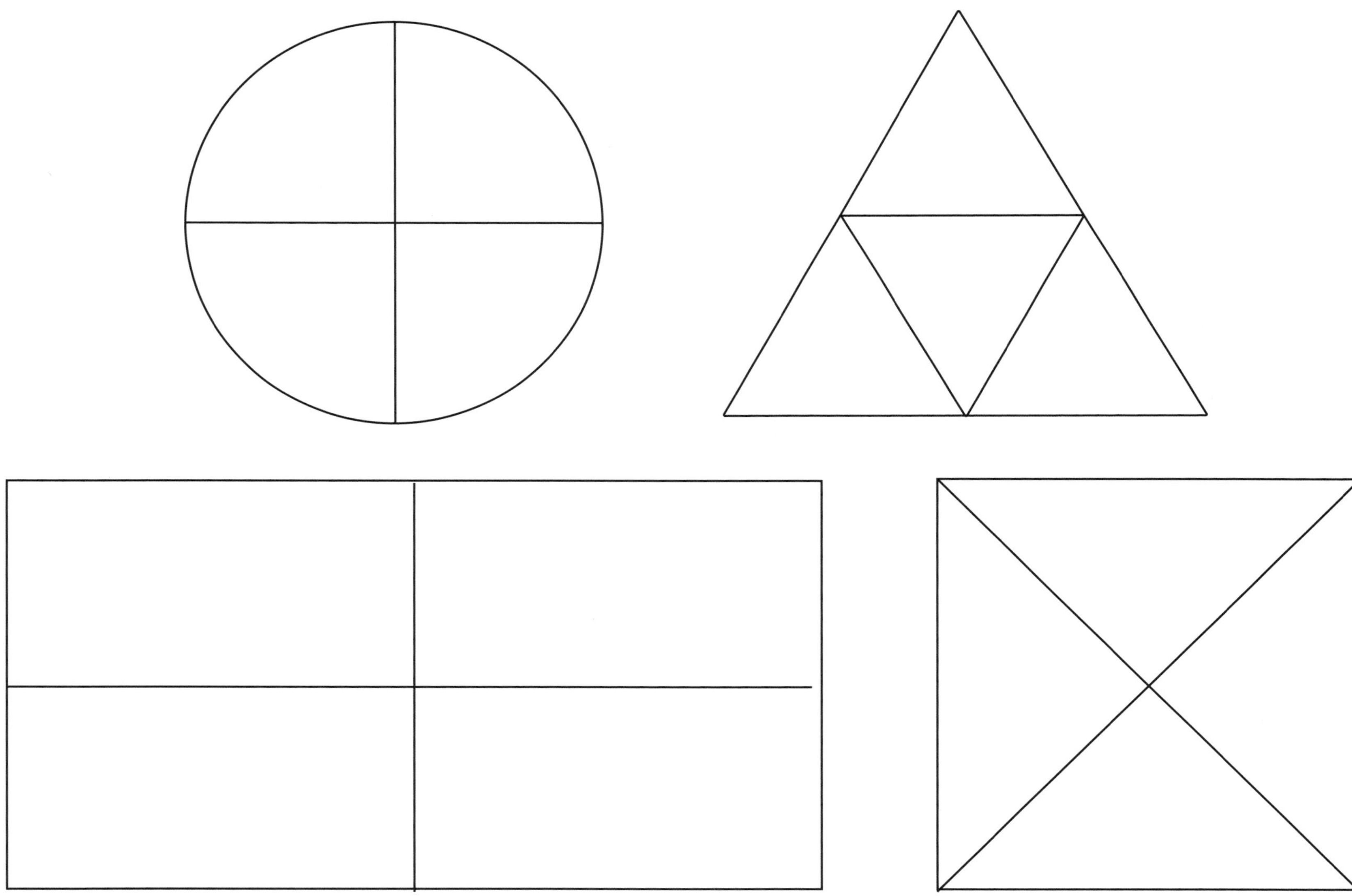

Race to 400

Maths focus: Adding two- and three-digit numbers.

A game for four to six players.

What you need:
- A set of dominoes (CD-ROM).
- Paper and pencil.
- Counters.

Instructions

1 Place a set of dominoes face down on the table and mix them up.
2 Players take it in turns to turn over a domino. Each domino makes two numbers. For example: if the domino turned over has a 4 and 3, it will makes 43 and 34.
3 Players add the two numbers to find their score,
4 for example: 43 + 34 = 77.
5 If a double domino is turned over, the score is double the number shown.
6 Players add their scores together after each turn. The first player to reach 400 or more is the winner.

Some players may find a set of place value cards helpful when adding their numbers together.

Dice differences

Maths focus: Subtracting pairs of two-digit numbers.

A game for two players.

What you need:
- The Dice differences player grids (p32).
- Two 1–6 dice (CD-ROM).
- Coloured pencils.

Instructions

1 Players take it in turns to roll both dice and use them to create two two-digit numbers.
2 The player's score is the difference between the two numbers. (From previous work, they will know that this is a multiple of 9.)
3 Players keep a running total of their score, crossing it off on their board.
4 If their score would take them beyond 99, the player misses that turn.
5 The first player to reach 99 is the winner.

Players can use the same board a number of times by using a different coloured pencil for each game. They could then play for 'best of five' games.

Dice differences

Player 1

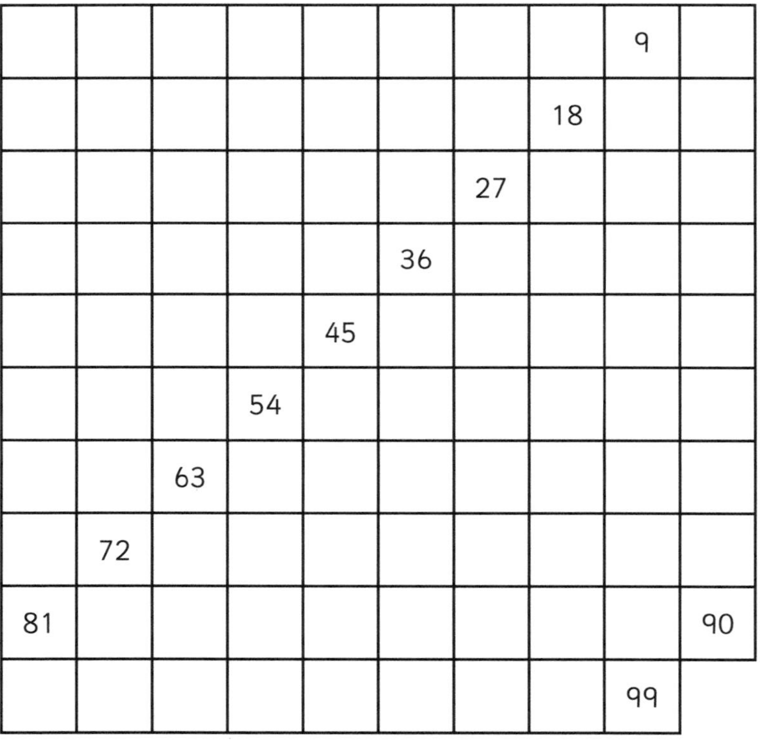

Player 2

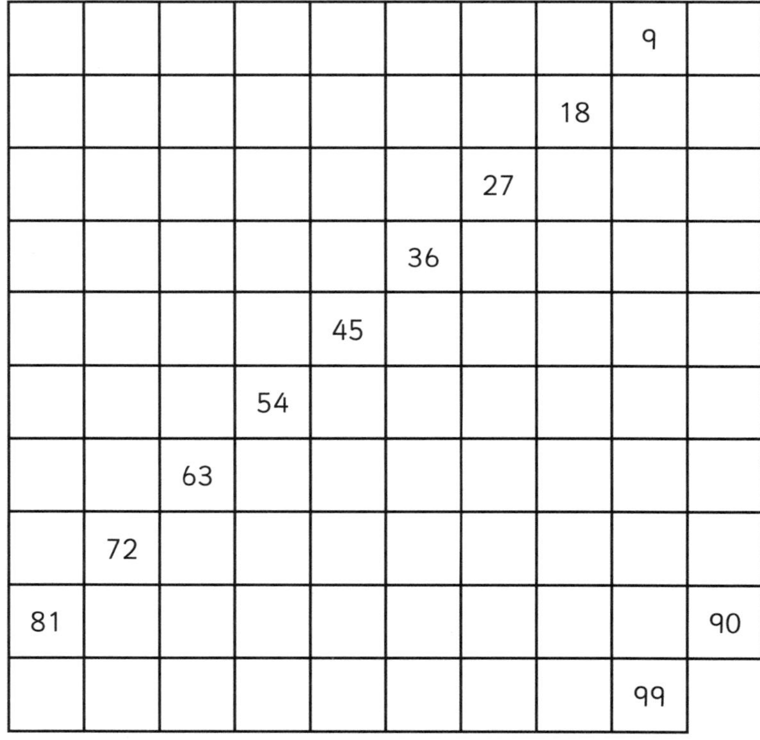

Only snakes

Maths focus: Multiplying single-digit and low two-digit numbers by 2, 3, 4, 5, 6, 9 and 10.

A game for two to four players.

What you need:

- The Only snakes game board (p34).
- Around 20 to 30 counters for each player, a different colour for each.

Instructions

The aim is for players to create a long snake of their own coloured counters on the Only snakes game board.

1 Players take it in turns to choose a number and say a multiplication calculation with that total.

2 The player claims the number by putting one of their coloured counters on it on the game board.

3 Players make strategic number choices, blocking other players' snakes, extending their own snakes or doing both at once.

4 The winner is the player with the longest snake when play stops. This could be after each player has used all their counters, after a particular length of time or when no more snakes can be made.

Only snakes

1	2	3	4	5	6	7	8	9	10
11	12	13	14	15	16	17	18	19	20
21	22	23	24	25	26	27	28	29	30
31	32	33	34	35	36	37	38	39	40
41	42	43	44	45	46	47	48	49	50
51	52	53	54	55	56	57	58	59	60
61	62	63	64	65	66	67	68	69	70
71	72	73	74	75	76	77	78	79	80
81	82	83	84	85	86	87	88	89	90
91	92	93	94	95	96	97	98	99	100

Shape, sort and cover

3Gg.01

Maths focus: Revising and consolidating 2D shape and associated vocabulary.

A game for two players

What you need:

- The Shape, sort and cover game board (p36).
- A set of coloured counters for each player.
- A 1–6 dice (CD-ROM).

Instructions: Game 1

1. Players take turns to throw the dice.
2. After each throw they put a counter on the board on a shape whose number of sides matches the number on the dice.
3. The winner is the player to get three of their counters in a straight line.

Instructions: Game 2

Play until the board is covered. The player with the most counters is the winner.

Instructions: Game 3

Players cannot place a counter until they name the shape that they have chosen, also saying one of the properties of that shape.

Teacher notes

At first, when playing the game, players may not have any idea of strategy. After a while, they may begin to develop strategies in order to block their opponent.

Some players may need more support, so use a second copy of the game board to make individual cards which can be matched to the shapes on the board. Players can sort them into sets according to the number of sides before the game starts. Then, when they have thrown the dice, they will have a limited number of shapes to choose from.

Shape, sort and cover

Across the swamp

Maths focus: To use the language of position, direction and movement and develop the understanding of compass points.

A game for two players.

What you need:

- The Across the swamp board (p38).
- A counter per player.
- A coin to toss.

Instructions: Game 1

1 Each player places their counter on their own explorer.

2 Players take turns to toss the coin.

3 If a 'head' is tossed, the explorer (counter) moves diagonally to the left (can be up or down).

4 If a 'tail' is tossed, the explorer moves diagonally to the right (up or down.)

5 If a player lands on a space which is shaded in some way, they follow the key below.

Key to shading:

Block: move one square north.

Stripe: move one square south.

Wavy line: move one square east.

Spots: move one square west.

6 Sometimes a player may be blocked, in which case they miss a turn.

7 The player who reaches the opposite explorer first is the winner.

Instructions: Game 2

1 Players keep a record of how many moves they make to reach the diagonally opposite corner.

2 The player who makes the least number of moves is the winner.

Teacher notes

Discuss which was the longest route and which was the shortest.

Work out which route would take the longest time and which would take the shortest. Would it be better to follow the four points of the compass or continue moving diagonally? Discuss the reasons why.

This game can be easily changed if the players want to bring their own rules to it. But make sure that the new rules are introduced before the game starts!

Across the swamp

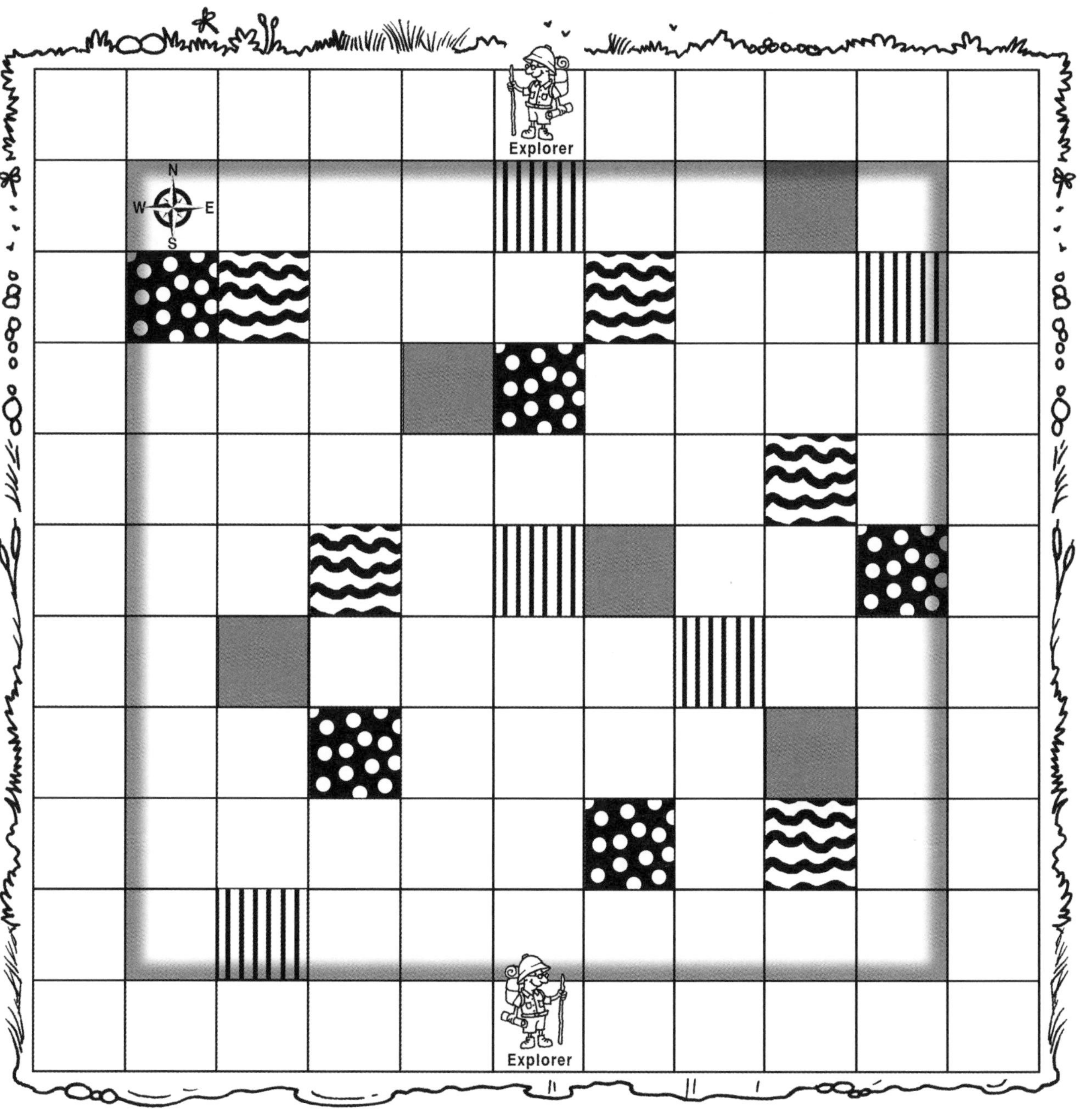

Build the pattern

Maths focus: Identify simple relationships between shapes, identify lines of symmetry.

A game for two players.

What you need:

- The Build the pattern game board (p40).
- The sheet of Build the pattern shape cards (p41).
- Scissors.
- 1–6 dice (CD-ROM).

Instructions: Game 1

Cut out the shape cards from the set on the sheet.

1 Players take turns to throw the dice and use the key on the game board to find the shape represented by the number they throw.

2 They then take that shape and place it on the board – they can either match a shape already there using the line of symmetry or place it in a new place, but the aim is to build a symmetrical pattern, so they must take care not to place a shape incorrectly.

3 All players must check that each shape is placed correctly. If it is not, the shape is removed and the player who placed it misses their next turn.

4 If it is impossible for a player to place the shape they have thrown, they miss that turn.

5 When there are no more spaces, the player who put in the last shape wins the game.

Instructions: Game 2

Play as for Game 1 but use two lines of symmetry.

Teacher notes

This game is a very visual and tactile one in which all players can achieve.

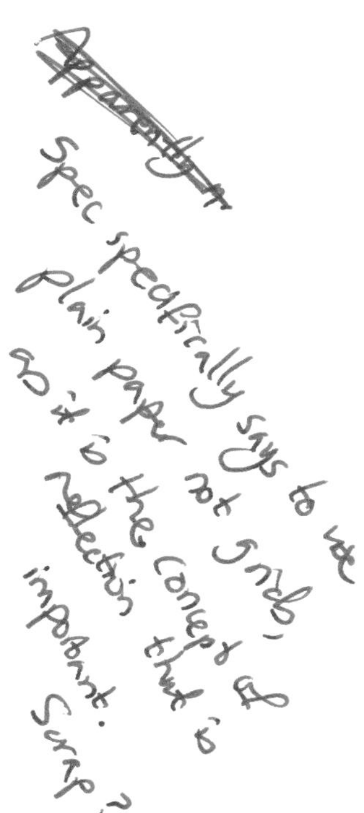

Build the pattern game board

Key:

1 and 6 = ■　　2 = ⬢

3 and 5 = ▲　　4 = ●

Build the pattern shape cards

Find the spider

4Gp.02

Maths focus: Find and describe the position of a square on a grid of squares where the rows and columns are labelled.

A game for two players.

What you need:

- A Find the Spider coordinate grid (p43) for each player.
- 1 set of Spiders (p43) per player.
- A 'barrier'.
- Five counters per player.

Instructions

1 Place the barrier between the players so they can't see each other's coordinate grid.

2 Each player places their spiders on their grid.

3 Players then take it in turns to say a coordinate to their partner.

4 When one player says a coordinate, the other player finds it on their own grid.

- If that coordinate is covered by a spider, they say 'found it' and place a counter on the spider.
- If the coordinate is not covered by a spider, or that spider already has a counter on it, no counter is placed and play continues.

5 The game ends when there is a counter on all of one player's spiders. That player loses the game.

Vary the game by using different combinations of different sized spiders. The smaller size will allow more to be placed on the board. Using five small spiders will make the game more difficult: there will be more spaces between spiders, so there will be less chance of a 'squash'.

Draw or tape a grid on the floor or outside and pay the game on a larger scale, using players to mark the coordinates.

Find the spider coordinate grids

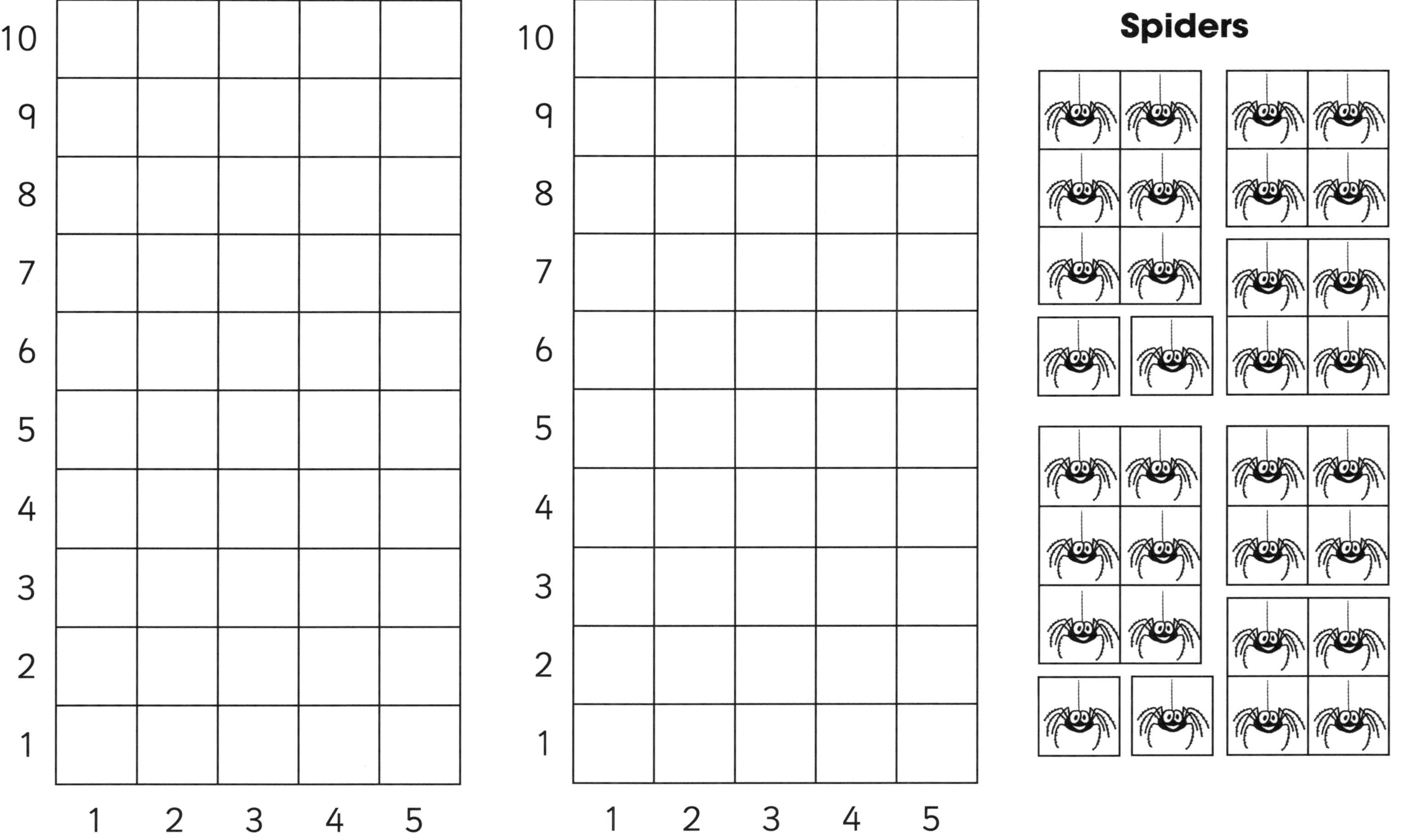

Spiders

Bank

Maths focus: Consolidation of money knowledge.
Use of addition facts up to 100.

A game for two to four players.

What you need:

- The Bank game board (p45).
- A selection of coins.
- Paper.
- Pencil for jotting.
- Paper clip for spinner.

Instructions: Game 1

1 Players take turns to spin the paper clip by holding it in the centre of the spinner with a pencil and flicking it.

2 They move that number of spaces and use coins to make up the value shown on the space.

3 If the value is correct, the player stays in place. If it is incorrect, they move back the number of spaces that they just moved.

4 The first player to land on 'finish' and correctly make up the value shown on that space in coins wins.

Instructions: Game 2

Play as before but challenge the players to make the amount shown with the least number of coins possible.

Teacher notes

This game is designed to consolidate and practise addition of money. It would be useful for players to have a good understanding of the different coins and their equivalence, but it is not necessary.

Some players may use lower values and then gradually include a process of trading them for higher values.

Bank

96¢ 88¢ 33¢ 13¢ 25¢ 99¢ 82¢ 64¢

55¢ 10¢

30¢ 43¢

47¢ 29¢

71¢ FINISH 24¢ 81¢

75¢ START 41¢ 60¢ 30¢ 17¢

1 2

Lose a turn 3

Time flies

Maths focus: Show the time to the nearest five minutes on an analogue clock and to the nearest minute on a digital clock; choose appropriate mental strategies to carry out calculations

A game for two to four players.

What you need:

- The Time flies game board (p47).
- A 1–6 dice (CD-ROM).
- One counter for each player.
- An analogue or digital clock for each player (or a sheet of paper and a pencil for each player).

Instructions: Game 1

1 Each player sets their clock to 12 o'clock.

2 Players take turns to throw the dice and move that number of places along the track.

3 As they land on a time section, they add the number of hours and/or minutes shown on the section to their clock.

4 Players continue playing until they have all reached the finish.

5 The winner is the player whose clock shows the latest time (in other words, the winner's clock will have had the most time added to the starting time of 12 o'clock).

For a more complex version of the game, each player has two counters on their home space and must get both to the finish, rolling a dice and moving one of their counters the matching number of spaces.

Instructions: Game 2

Play as for Game 1, but if a player lands on a section with flies, they spend the same amount of time in minutes as there are flies, swatting them.

Teacher notes

This involves taking time off their clocks.

If analogue clocks are used, each player will need a clock with hands that are geared. This ensures that as the minute hand moves, the hour hand moves at the correct rate. Cardboard clocks with independent hands will not be helpful for this game.

This game is designed to reinforce the concept of the passage of time. As players move around the board they collect units of time. This can be done using an analogue or a digital clock.

Some players may want to add the times as they play, others may write the times and total them at the end. It is best to let each player choose which the best way is for them

Time flies

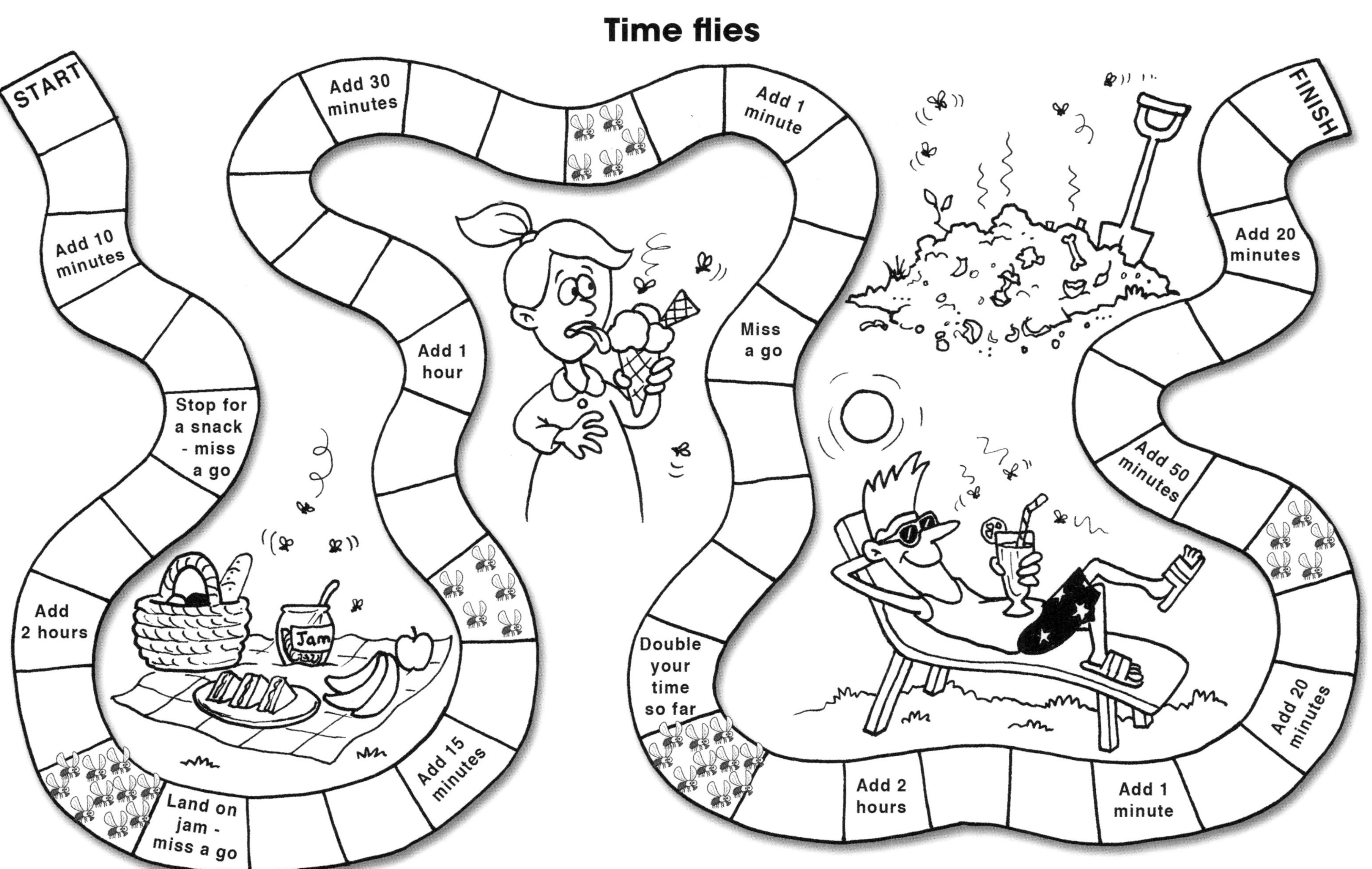
START
Add 10 minutes
Stop for a snack - miss a go
Add 2 hours
Land on jam - miss a go
Add 15 minutes
Add 1 hour
Add 30 minutes
Add 1 minute
Miss a go
Double your time so far
Add 2 hours
Add 1 minute
Add 20 minutes
Add 50 minutes
Add 20 minutes
FINISH
Jam

How long will it take?

Maths focus: Begin to calculate simple time intervals in hours and minutes.

A game for two to four players.

What you need:

- The How long will it take? game board (p49).
- Counters (one per player).
- A 1–6 dice (CD-ROM).
- A set of How long will it take? time cards (p50).

Instructions

The aim of the game is to collect the least amount of time on the journey home.

1 Players place their counter on a house on the game board and must reach the house diagonally opposite.

2 They take turns to throw the dice and move in any direction.
   - If they land on a time, they take a matching time card.
   - If they land on a stripy section, they have another go.
   - If they land on a shaded section, they miss a turn.

3 When all players have finished, they total the amount of time they have collected.

4 The player with the least amount of time is the winner.

Teacher notes

This is a game of chance but also of strategy. When they first play the game, players may want to get to the end first – but this is not a game for racing! The idea is to find a route that gives the least amount of time. The more players play the game, the more they will use the idea of strategy, using their moves to work round the board collecting the least amount of time.

Some players may need a clock when adding their time at the end of the game. This will be a visual way of experiencing the passing of time.

How long will it take?

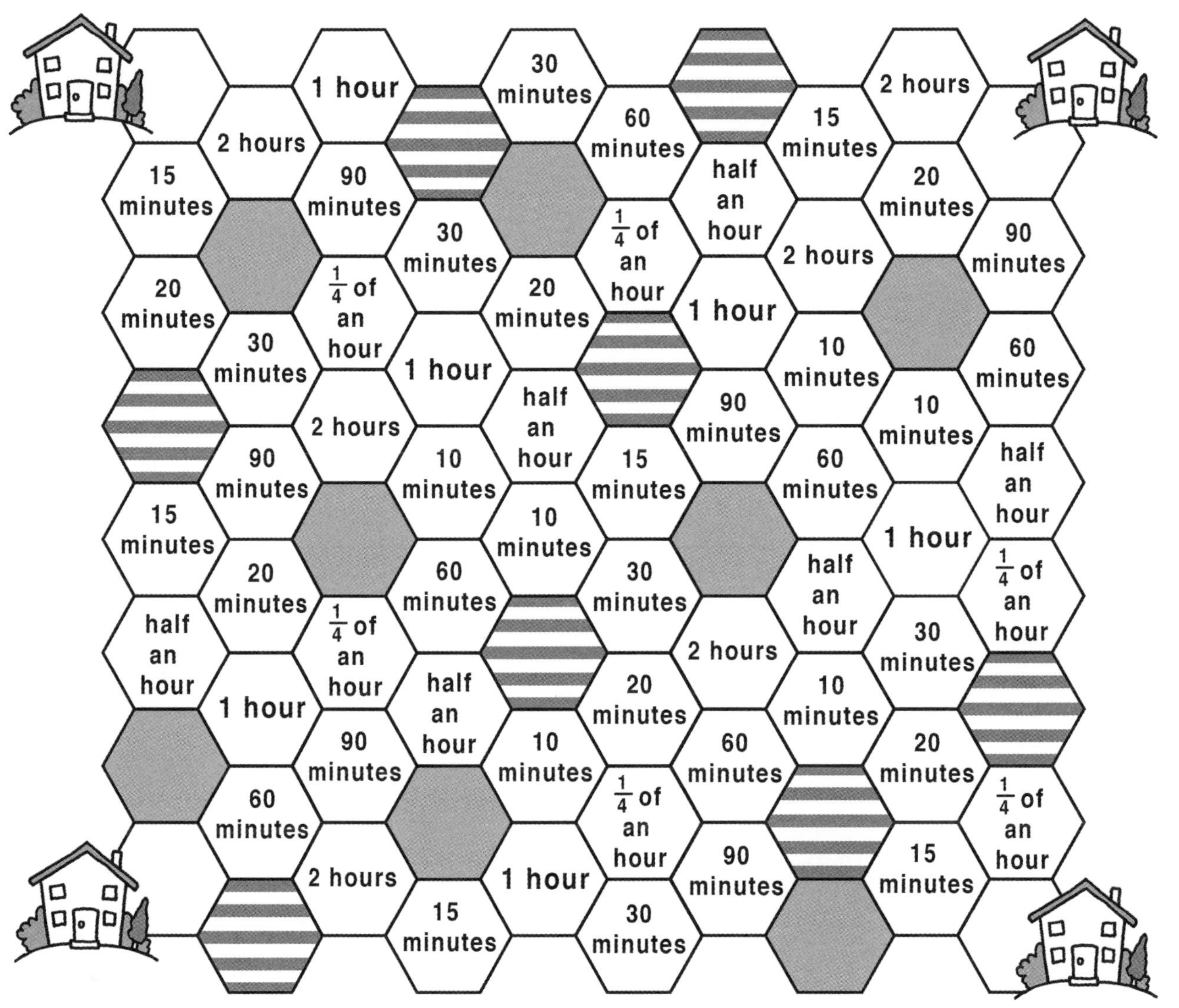

How long will it take? time cards

1 hour	15 minutes	60 minutes	30 minutes	half an hour = 30 minutes
$\frac{1}{4}$ of an hour = 15 minutes	2 hours	90 minutes	20 minutes	10 minutes
1 hour	15 minutes	60 minutes	30 minutes	half an hour = 30 minutes
$\frac{1}{4}$ of an hour = 15 minutes	2 hours	90 minutes	20 minutes	10 minutes
1 hour	15 minutes	60 minutes	30 minutes	half an hour = 30 minutes
$\frac{1}{4}$ of an hour = 15 minutes	2 hours	90 minutes	20 minutes	10 minutes
1 hour	15 minutes	60 minutes	30 minutes	half an hour = 30 minutes
$\frac{1}{4}$ of an hour = 15 minutes	2 hours	90 minutes	20 minutes	10 minutes
1 hour	15 minutes	60 minutes	30 minutes	half an hour = 30 minutes
$\frac{1}{4}$ of an hour = 15 minutes	2 hours	90 minutes	20 minutes	10 minutes
1 hour	15 minutes	60 minutes	30 minutes	half an hour = 30 minutes
$\frac{1}{4}$ of an hour = 15 minutes	2 hours	90 minutes	20 minutes	10 minutes

Calendar game

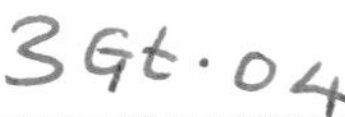

Maths focus: Write number sentences using all four operations; read a calendar and calculate time intervals in weeks or days.

A game for two to four players.

What you need:
- A pack of playing cards.
- Calendar pages (one per player).
- Counters to cover the dates (a different colour per player).
- A one or two minute sand timer.

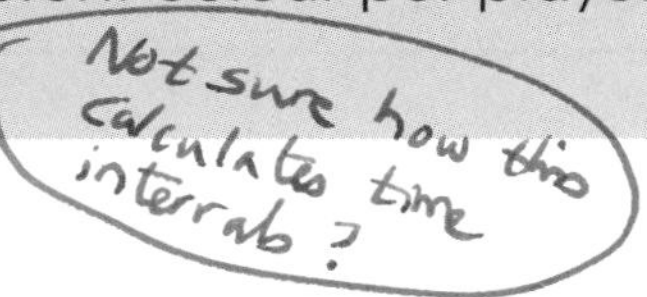

Instructions

1 Players take it in turns to hold up two playing cards.

2 All the players then write as many different number sentences using the numbers on the cards as they can within one minute (or two minutes). Both cards must be used.

For example, if the two cards are a 4 and a 6, players can write the following number sentences:

$6 + 4 = 10$ or $4 + 6 = 10$, $6 - 4 = 2$, $6 \times 4 = 24$ or $4 \times 6 = 24$.

(Jacks = 11, Queens = 12, Kings = 13, Aces can be used as 1 or 0).

3 Each player places a counter on their calendar page over the numbers they made.

4 When 10 dates have been covered, players show three cards each time. All the cards must be used in each number sentence.

5 The game ends when no more dates can be made.

Challenge question: When will that be? What numbers can't be made?

Matching measures

Maths focus: Choose appropriate units for measuring length, weight and capacity.

A game for two to four players.

What you need:
- Two sets of Matching measures – picture cards (pp52–54).
- Two sets of Matching measures – measure cards (pp55–57).
- Scissors.

Instructions

1 Cut out all the cards.

2 Shuffle the set of picture cards and the set of measure cards separately and place them face down in two piles between the players.

3 Players take turns to take the top card from each pile.

4 If the picture card matches its appropriate measure card (e.g. the picture card showing something – pencil, book etc.– which would be measured in centimetres and the measure card shows 'centimetre'), they place them next to them as a pair.

5 Any cards that do not match are left face up on the table. A player may use the face up cards to match with any they turn over.

6 When there are no cards left in the packs, the player with most paired cards is the winner.

Teacher notes

This game allows players to use their knowledge of measures in a fun way. It develops further understanding of measures, when they would be used and the abbreviations used for each one.

Matching measures cards – picture cards 1

Matching measures cards – picture cards 2

Matching measures cards – picture cards 3

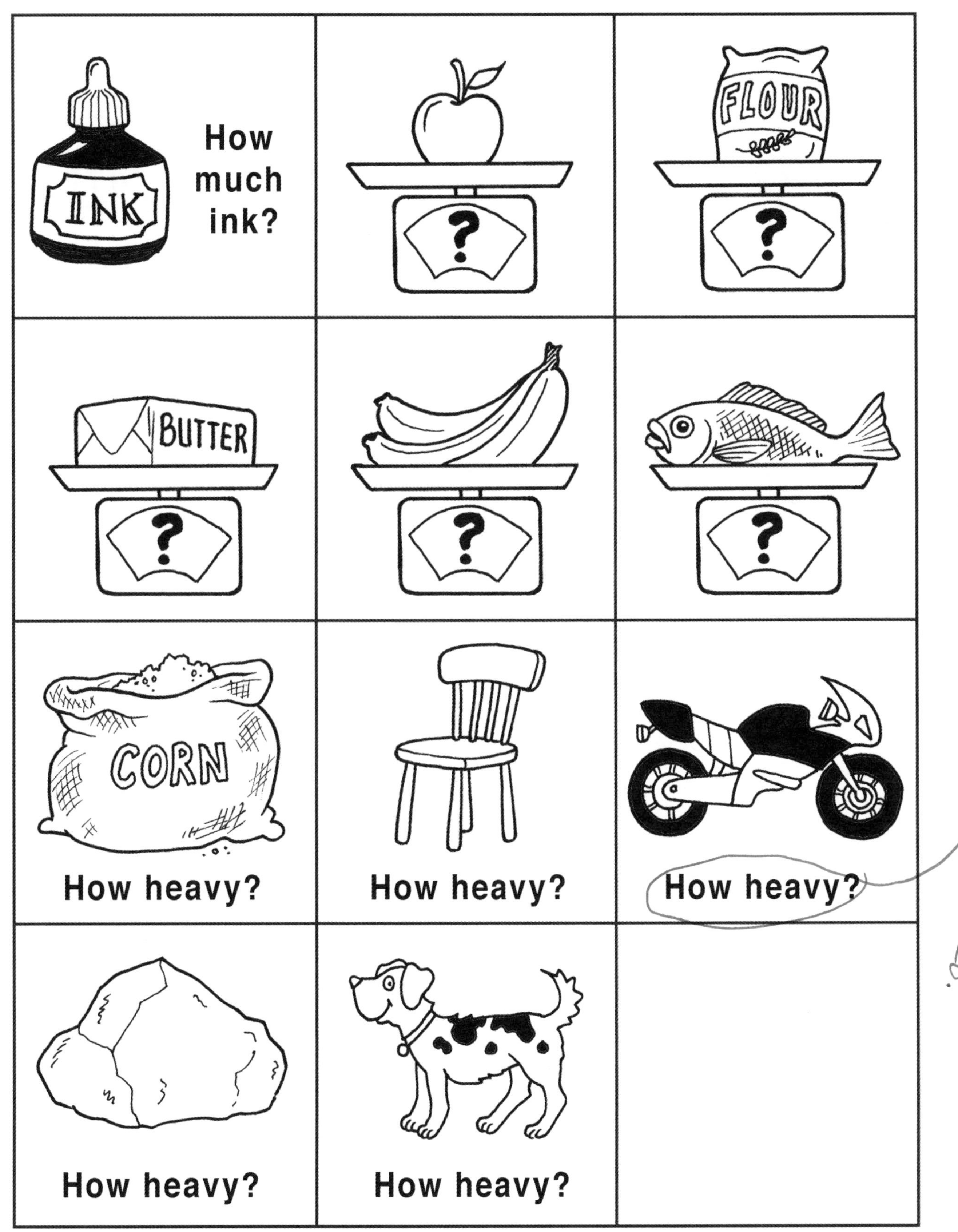

Matching measures cards – measure cards 1

centimetres	centimetres	centimetres
centimetres	centimetres	metres
metres	metres	metres
metres	kilometres	kilometres

Matching measures cards - measure cards 2

kilometres	kilometres	kilometres
litres	litres	litres
litres	litres	millilitres
millilitres	millilitres	millilitres

Matching measures cards – measure cards 3

millilitres	grams	grams
grams	grams	litres
kilograms	kilograms	kilograms
kilograms	kilograms	

How much will you have to spend?

Maths focus: Recognise the value of coins, exchange coins of equivalent values, and make change.

A game for two players.

What you need:

- The How much will you have to spend? (p59) game board.
- A How much will you have to spend? change sheet (p60).
- Coins with a total of $2.00 for each player.
- A 1–6 dice (CD-ROM).
- One counter per player.
- A pot containing coins with a total of $5.00.
  Note that the coins should include some 25c and 50c coins, but also plenty of low value to ensure players can make change as required.

Instructions: Game 1

Each player starts with $2.00.

The aim of the game is to collect the most money to spend at the zoo.

1 Players take turns to throw the dice and move that number of places.
2 If they land on a money section they pick up the amount it says (take it from the pot) or drop the amount it says (put it in the pot). They may need to give change (taking a larger amount from the pot and putting some of their own money back in) or vice versa. If necessary they can ask their opponent to swap some coins (e.g. put 5 × 1c coins in the pot and take a 5c coin out).
3 If it is not possible to pick up or drop the relevant amount, the player misses that turn.
4 Players can choose their own route, but cannot travel round the same section of the track more than once.
5 When they reach the zoo gates, players total their money. The winner is the player with the most money.

Instructions: Game 2

Play as for Game 1 but use larger amounts of money so players are more likely to need to work out change.

Teacher notes

Some players may need smaller value coins than others.

At the beginning, players will play this as a game of chance. The more they play the more they will use the idea of strategy and plan their route according to the number thrown.

Some players may need to use the change sheet to help them when giving change or making larger amounts to total.

How much will you have to spend?

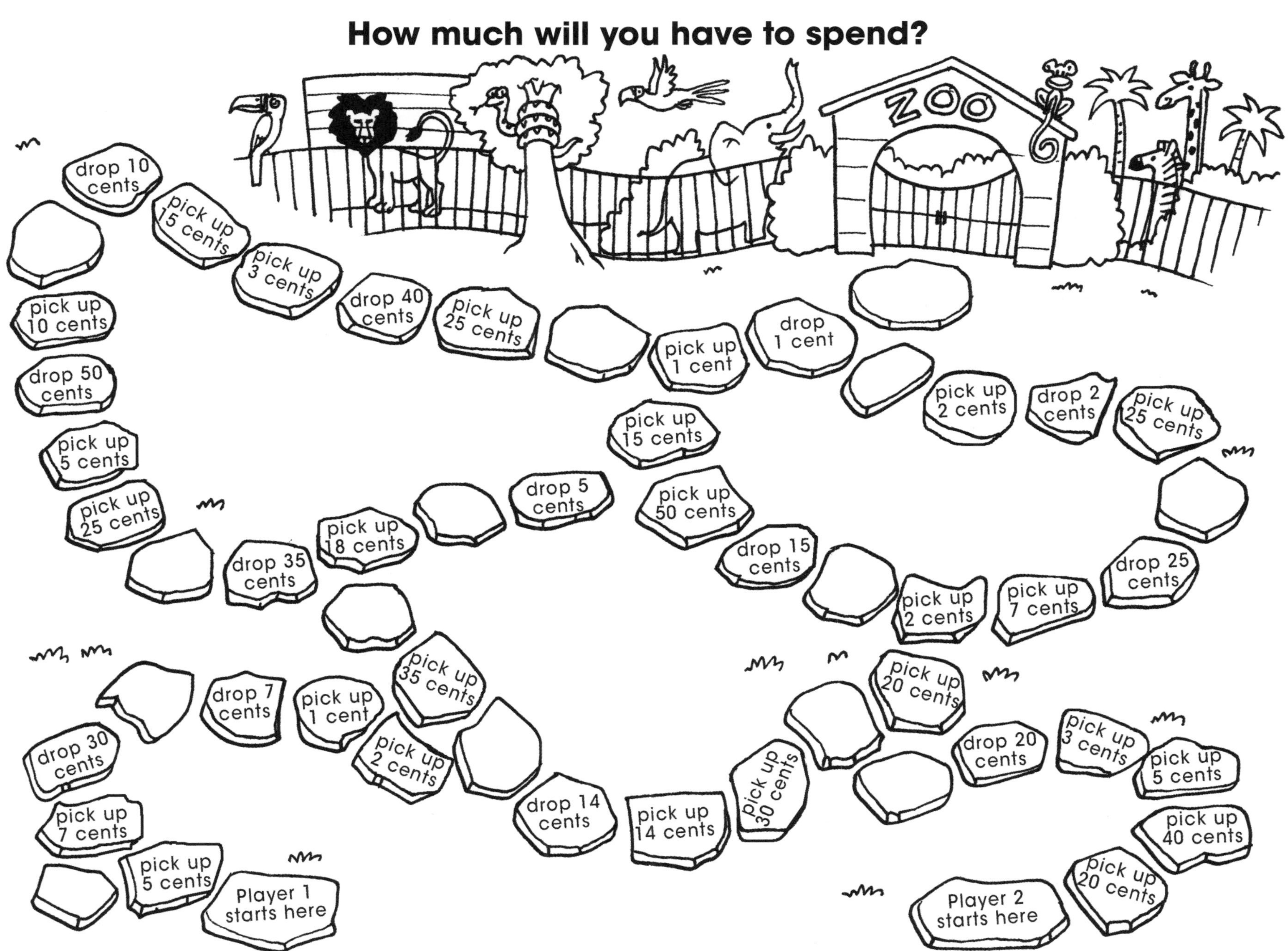

How much will you have to spend? change sheet

1¢	1c	1c	1c	1c	1c	=	5¢
5¢	5c	5c				=	10¢
10¢	10c	10c	10c			=	25¢
25¢	25c	25c	25c	25c		=	$

1¢	1c	1c	1c	1c	1c	=	5¢
5¢	5c	5c				=	10¢
10¢	10c	10c	10c			=	25¢
25¢	25c	25c	25c	25c		=	$

1¢	1c	1c	1c	1c	1c	=	5¢
5¢	5c	5c				=	10¢
10¢	10c	10c	10c			=	25¢
25¢	25c	25c	25c	25c		=	$

Read the clocks

Maths focus: Read the time on analogue and digital clocks, to the nearest five minutes on an analogue clock and to the nearest minute on a digital clock.

A game for two to four players.

What you need:

- The Read the clocks game board (p62).
- A set of Read the clocks time cards (1) and (2) (pp63–64).
- One counter per player.
- A 1–6 dice (CD-ROM).
- Scissors.
- Glue.

Instructions: Game 1

1 Shuffle the time cards and place one card on each numbered space on the track, clock side up.

2 Players take turns to roll the dice and move that number of spaces round the board.

3 Players pick up the time card they land on. They say the time it shows and check by looking on the back.

- If they are correct, they move forward the number of spaces shown under the card.
- If they are incorrect, they move back the number of spaces under the card.
- They don't take another time card until after their next throw of the dice.

4 They then replace the card.

5 If they land on a shaded square, they miss that turn.

6 The first player to get to 'Finish' is the winner.

Instructions: Game 2

Play as for Game 1, but if a player gets the time wrong, they put the card in a pile in the space indicated at the bottom of the track after moving back.

If a player lands on a shaded section they can **either** stay where they are **or** choose a card from one of the piles at the bottom of the track. If they get the time right, they put the card back in the pile and move on four spaces; if they get it wrong, they put the card back in the pile and move back four spaces.

Teacher notes

This game gives players opportunities to read both analogue and digital times. Players will check the readings of each other's cards.

Game 2 will also use decision making.

For less confident players, the game can be played as pairs against pairs. This will allow discussion between the players.

Read the clocks game board

Start		6	5	6		4	5			Finish
1		4		3		3		1		1
2		4		6		6		2		2
3		1				5		4		3
		2		1		1		3		
5		5		2		6		5		5
6				2		6		6		6
3		3		4	5			2		1
1		6						3		3
5	2	4		Analogue time cards		Digital time cards		1	1	4

Read the clocks time cards (1)

	a quarter past twelve		ten o'clock		five to eight
	two o'clock		half past eleven		twenty past eight
	five to four		ten to one		twenty-five past nine
	twenty-five to five		five past one		twenty-five past ten
	twenty-five past five		a quarter past two		a quarter to twelve
	six o'clock		ten past three		twenty to one
	ten past seven		half past four		five past four
	a quarter past eight		a quarter to six		twenty-five to ten
	twenty to ten		ten to seven	19:26	seven twenty-six
01:11	one eleven	10:14	ten fourteen	20:15	eight fifteen
02:50	two fifty	11:13	eleven thirteen	21:00	nine o'clock
03:44	three forty-four	12:48	twelve forty-eight	22:53	ten fifty-three
04:01	four oh-one	13:37	one thirty-seven	23:23	eleven twenty-three

Read the clocks time cards (2)

05:15	five fifteen	14:05	two oh-five	00:07	twelve oh-seven
06:51	six fifty-one	15:21	three twenty-one	07:39	seven thirty-nine
07:42	seven forty-two	16:58	four fifty-eight	20:00	eight o'clock
08:24	eight twenty-four	17:45	five forty-five	17:53	five fifty-three
09:10	nine ten	18:33	six thirty-three		

Clean up the money

Maths focus: Learners use their knowledge of coordinates and money notation. They make sensible estimates and use addition facts in the context of money.

A game for two players.

What you need:
- The Clean up the money game board (p66).
- A 1–6 dice (CD-ROM).
- A selection of coins from 1c to $1, 36 in total.

Instructions

1 Place the coins randomly on the board, one coin in each space.

2 Each player takes a turn to throw the dice twice.
The first throw shows the horizontal position of the coordinates and the second throw shows the vertical.

3 The player collects the coin that is in that space.

4 If there is no coin, that player misses a turn.
Play continues until there are six coins left on the board.

5 Players total the amount of money they have.

6 The player with the most money is the winner.

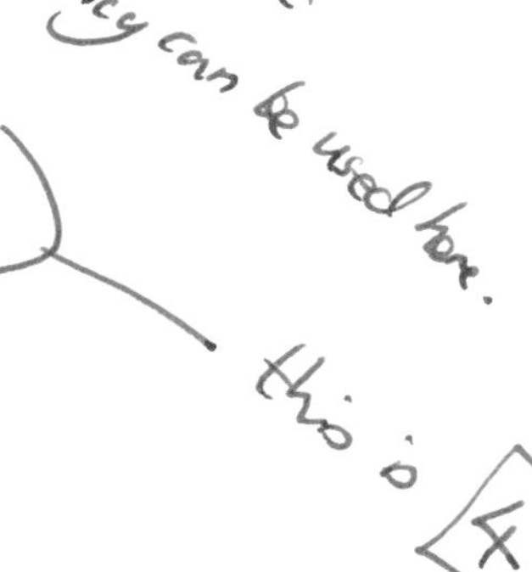

How to play Game 2

Play as for Game 1 but each player throws two dice at the same time. This can be used strategically as the player works out the two possible coordinates and chooses the one that will give the most money.

Teacher notes

Because of the random nature of the dice, each game will give different totals. Some players may need to use a 100 square to help with addition.

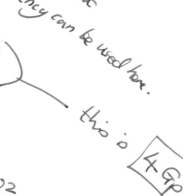

Clean up the money

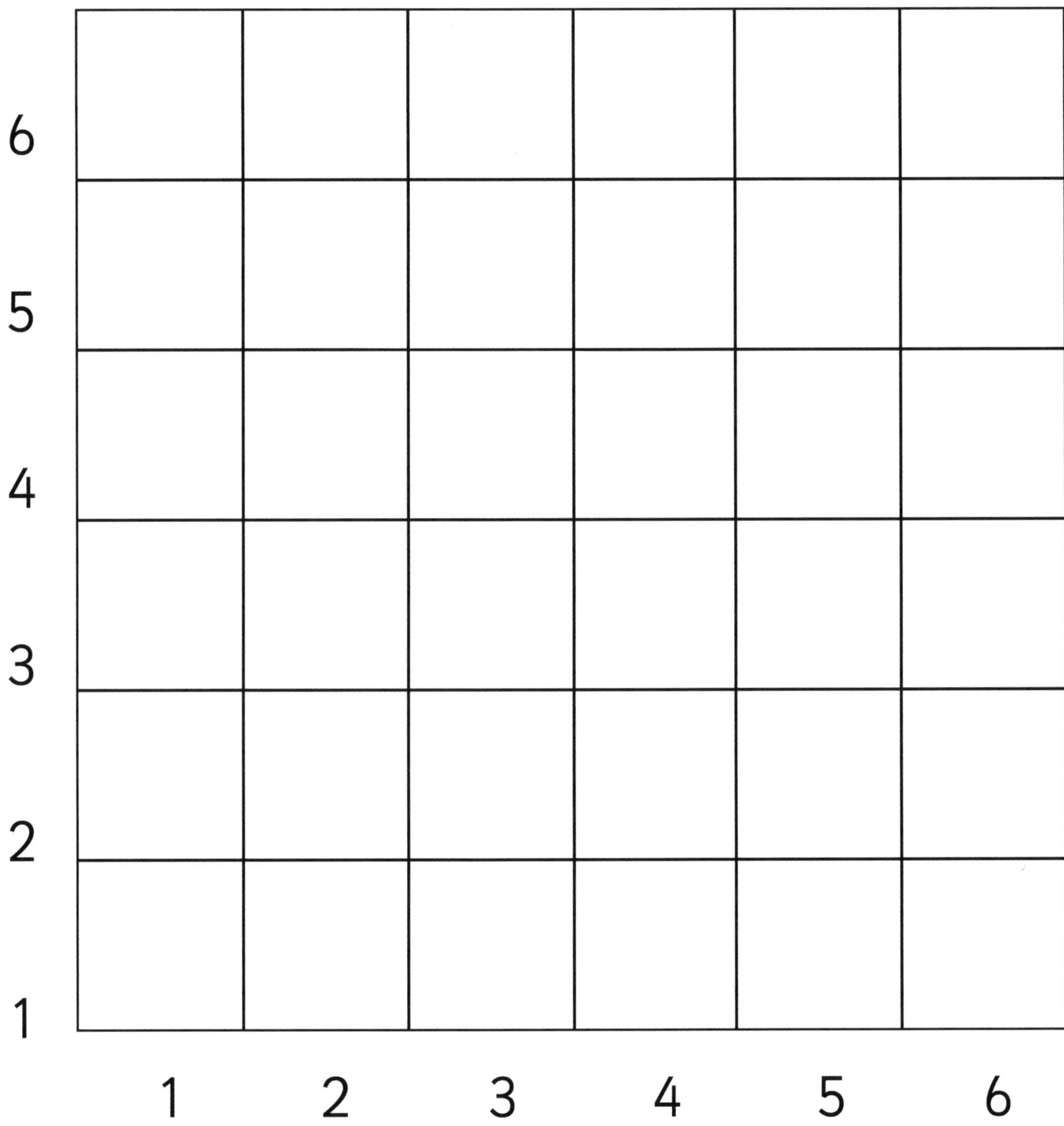

Milking the goats

Maths focus: Use the relationship between litres and millilitres.

A game for two to four players.

What you need:

- The Milking the goats game board (p68).
- One Milking the goats recording jug (p69) per player.
- A 1–6 dice (CD-ROM).
- One counter per player.

Instructions: Game 1

1 Players place their counters on 'Start: Monday'.

2 They then take turns to roll the dice and move the number of spaces thrown.

3 The first square they land on tells them how much milk they collect on Monday. They mark this on their recording jug.

4 They then move their counters to the 'Tuesday' square.

5 On their next turn, the square they land on tells them how much milk they collect on Tuesday. They mark this on their recording jug, adding it to what they collected on Monday.

6 They then move their counters to the 'Wednesday' square, and so on until the end of the week.

7 The winner is the player with the most whole litres at the end of the week. If there is a tie, add on the remaining ml.

Instructions: Game 2

Play as for Game 1, but travel round the whole track, collecting more than one amount of milk each day.

Teacher notes

Goats only get milked once a day, but for Game 2, if a player lands within the same day, they can milk a different goat!

Game 2 gives players the opportunity to collect more milk and change it to litres.

Some players may like to go twice round the track.

The score sheets can be laminated and reused, using washable pens.

Milking the goats game board

Milking the goats recording jugs

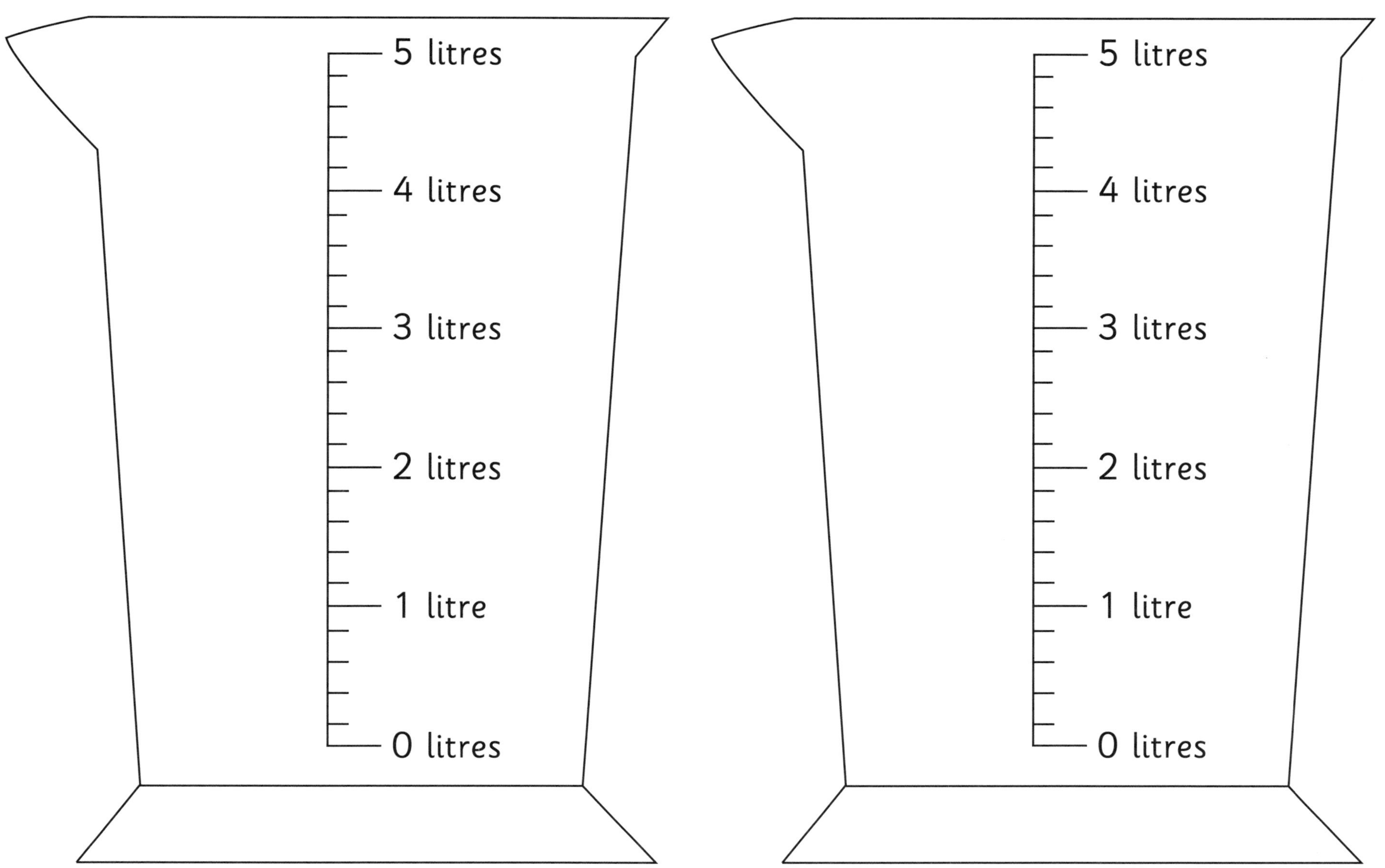

Round the track 3Gg·02

Maths focus: Use the relationship between metres and centimetres.

A game for two to four players.

What you need:
- The Round the track game board (p71).
- A Round the track recording sheet (p72).
- A 1–6 Dice (CD-ROM).
- One counter per player.

Instructions: Game 1

1 Players place their counter on any corner of the track.

2 Players then take turns to throw the dice and move that number of spaces.

3 If they land on a shaded area, they follow the 'How to play' in the centre of the board to find their distance for that event in centimetres. (Depending on the numbers they throw, players may not land on a particular shaded area.) They write their distance on their recording sheet.

4 Players must visit every event, but can go round the track more than once.

5 When all players have finished, they total their distances. The winner is the player with the longest distance.

Instructions: Game 2

Play as for Game 1 but visit each event twice.

Instructions: Game 3

Play as before but players must visit each event in order – if they go beyond an event, they can move backwards on their next go. Award a bonus of 50 cm for the player who completes each event first, and/or for the player who completes the whole track first.

Teacher notes

This game can be played by players of all abilities. It is a game of chance that allows players to work out amounts in cm and convert them to metres and centimetres.

Some players may need to use a calculator to find their scores.

Encourage players to talk to each other to discuss what they have found out and to share strategies for finding totals.

Round the track

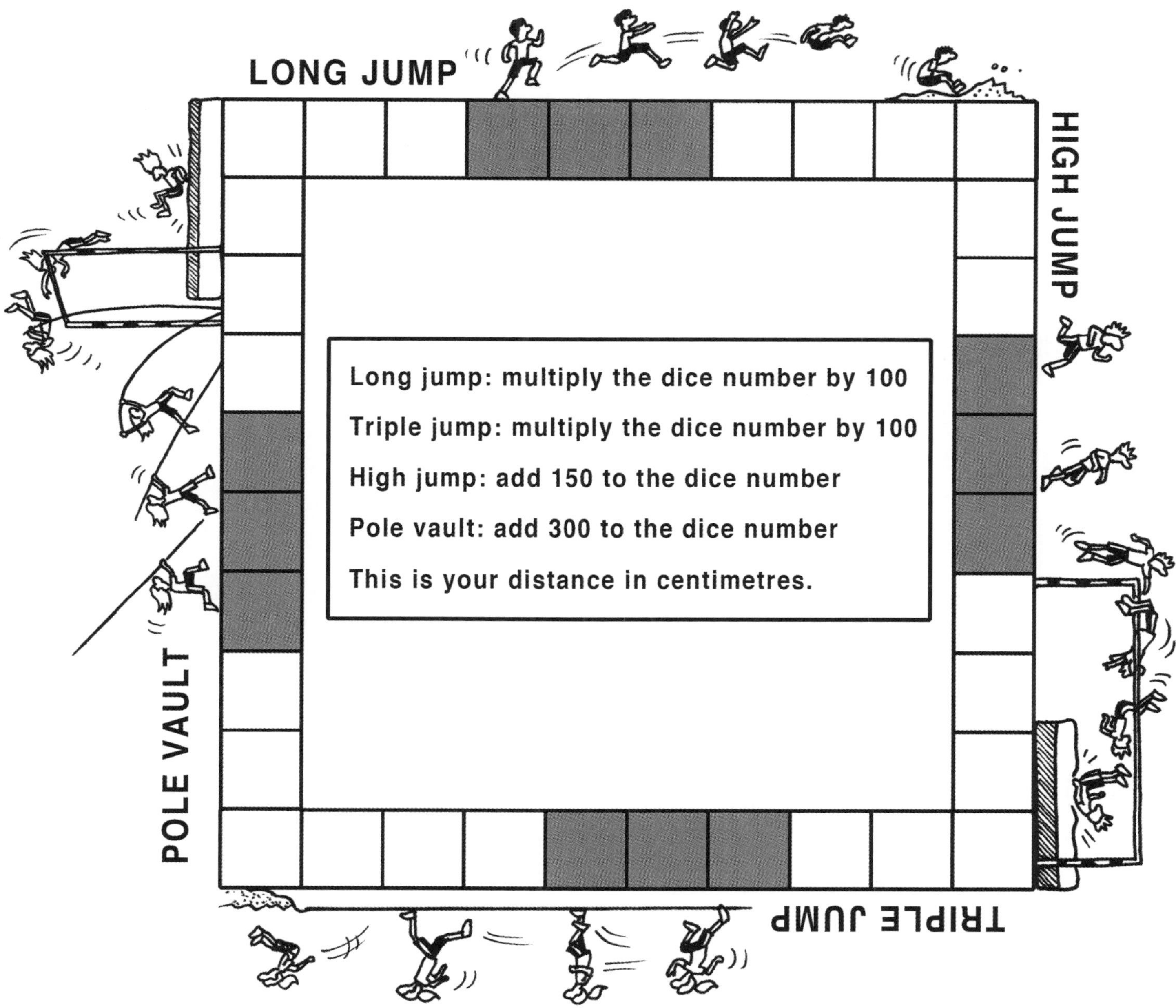

LONG JUMP
HIGH JUMP
TRIPLE JUMP
POLE VAULT
Long jump: multiply the dice number by 100
Triple jump: multiply the dice number by 100
High jump: add 150 to the dice number
Pole vault: add 300 to the dice number
This is your distance in centimetres.

Round the track recording sheets

	metres	cm
Long jump		
High jump		
Pole vault		
Triple jump		
Total		

	metres	cm
Long jump		
High jump		
Pole vault		
Triple jump		
Total		

	metres	cm
Long jump		
High jump		
Pole vault		
Triple jump		
Total		

	metres	cm
Long jump		
High jump		
Pole vault		
Triple jump		
Total		

	metres	cm
Long jump		
High jump		
Pole vault		
Triple jump		
Total		

	metres	cm
Long jump		
High jump		
Pole vault		
Triple jump		
Total		

Harvest time

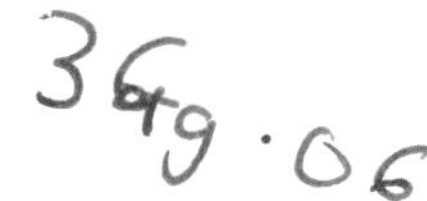

Maths focus: Use the relationship between kilograms and grams.

A game for two to four players.

What you need:

- The Harvest time game board (p74).
- Harvest time game weight cards (p75).
- Players' Harvest time weight cards and sack card (p76) (one per player).
- 1–6 dice (CD-ROM).
- Counter per player,
- Paper and pencil.

Instructions: Game 1

1 Shuffle the game weight cards and put them in their space at the centre of the board.

2 Each player arranges their own weight cards in their sack and puts their counter on one of the 'Start' squares.

3 Players take turns to throw the dice and move that number of spaces.

- If a player lands on a 'spill' space, they take that much out of their sack and add it to the pile in the centre of the board.
- If they do not have a card showing the correct amount, they can use two or more cards which add to the correct total.
- If they land on a 'Collect' space, they take a matching card from the centre of the board and add it to their sack.

4 When all players have reached 'Finish', they total the amount of weight in their sack in kilograms.

5 The winner is the player with the most whole kilos. If there is a tie, add the spare grams.

Instructions: Game 2

Players make and play their own version of this game, using grams and kilos.

Teacher notes

Although this game is a game of chance, some strategy can be built in. As all paths have chances to spill corn, the shortest path has the highest probability of landing on one of them. Some players may work that out and want to start on the longest path.

Some players may need to use a calculator for converting grams to kilos, but should not need one for the addition of grams.

If players make their own games, use time in the school day so that other players can play them. Challenge them to make an easier game, or a harder game.

Harvest time

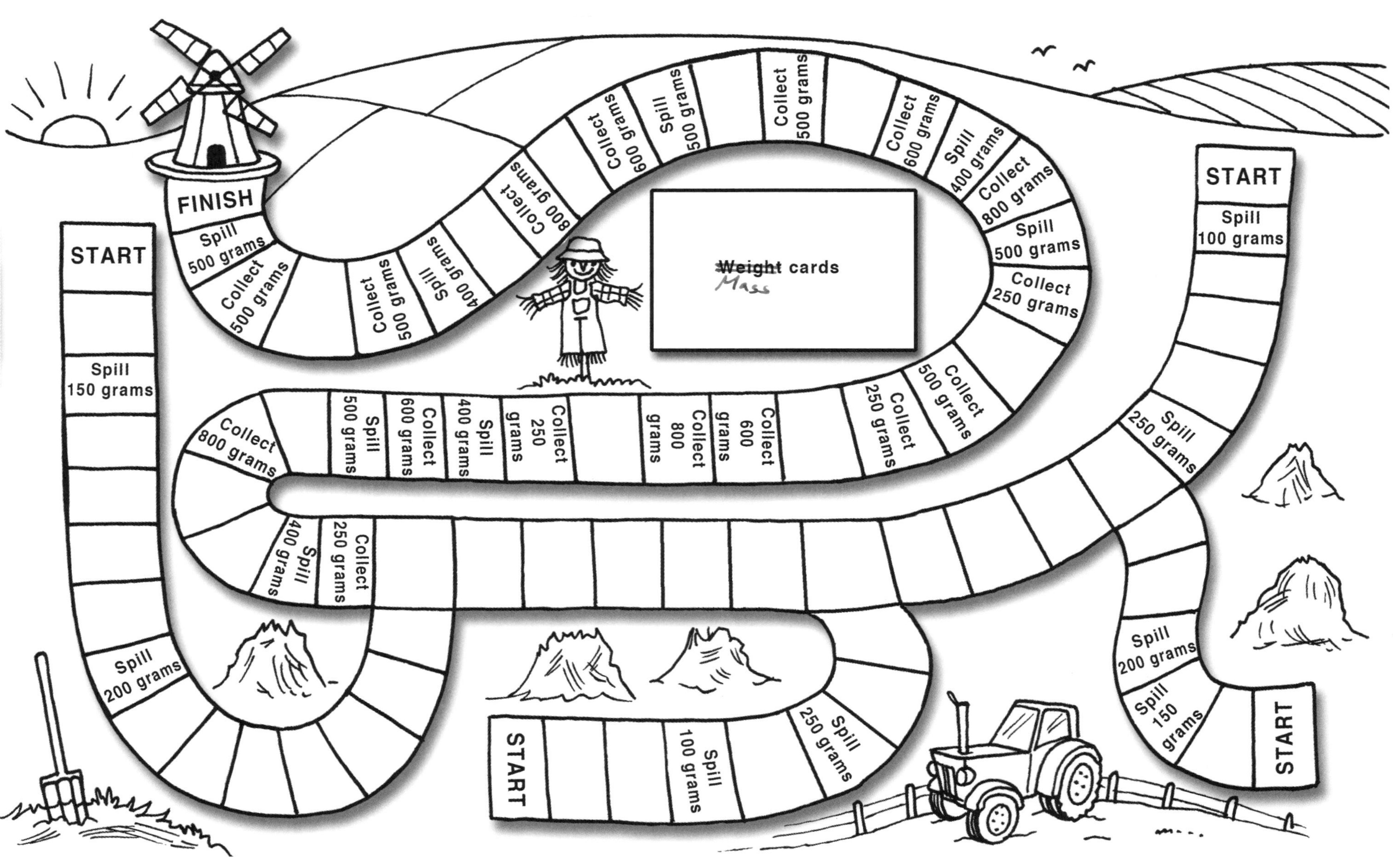

Harvest time: game ~~weight~~ mass cards

(for the centre of the board)

500 grams	250 grams	800 grams	600 grams
500 grams	250 grams	800 grams	600 grams
500 grams	250 grams	800 grams	600 grams
500 grams	250 grams	800 grams	600 grams
500 grams	250 grams	800 grams	600 grams
500 grams	250 grams	800 grams	600 grams
500 grams	250 grams	800 grams	600 grams
500 grams	250 grams	800 grams	600 grams
500 grams	250 grams	800 grams	600 grams
500 grams	250 grams	800 grams	600 grams
500 grams	250 grams	800 grams	600 grams
500 grams	250 grams	800 grams	600 grams
500 grams	250 grams	800 grams	600 grams
500 grams	250 grams	800 grams	600 grams
500 grams	250 grams	800 grams	600 grams
500 grams	250 grams	800 grams	600 grams

Harvest time: players' weight cards and sack card

100 grams	100 grams	
100 grams	150 grams	
200 grams	200 grams	
200 grams	250 grams	
250 grams	250 grams	
300 grams	400 grams	
400 grams	400 grams	
500 grams	500 grams	

100 grams	100 grams	
100 grams	150 grams	
200 grams	200 grams	
200 grams	250 grams	
250 grams	250 grams	
300 grams	400 grams	
400 grams	400 grams	
500 grams	500 grams	

A walk in the park: what do you see?

Maths focus: Use pictograms to represent data.

A game for two to four players.

What you need:

- A walk in the park: what do you see? game board (p78).
- A walk in the park: what do you see? base grid (p79).
- A walk in the park: what do you see? picture cards (p80).
- A walk in the park: what do you see? large picture cards (p80).
- A 1–6 dice (CD-ROM).
- One counter per player.

Instructions: Game 1

1. Shuffle the four Large picture cards and place them face down.
2. Players place their counters on the park gates.
3. They take turns to throw the dice and move that number of spaces.
4. Whatever picture they land on, they take a matching Picture card and place it on their Base grid, making a pictogram.
5. If a player lands on a bench, they miss a turn.
6. The game ends when all the players are back at the park gates.
7. Players then turn over the Large picture card.
8. Whoever has most of that picture on their Base grid is the winner.

Instructions: Game 2

Play as for Game 1, but make each symbol worth two.

Players add the totals for all their symbols and the winner is the one with the highest total.

Teacher notes

This game allows players to use what they know about pictograms in order to find the winner.

It is a game of chance and the result could be different every time the game is played.

It is a very visual game that all levels of ability can play. The resulting pictogram does not need the ability to count, as the longest line of symbols matching the card means more, and therefore will show the winner.

A walk in the park: what do you see?

A walk in the park: what do you see? Base grid

A walk in the park: what do you see? Picture cards

A walk in the park: what do you see? Large picture cards

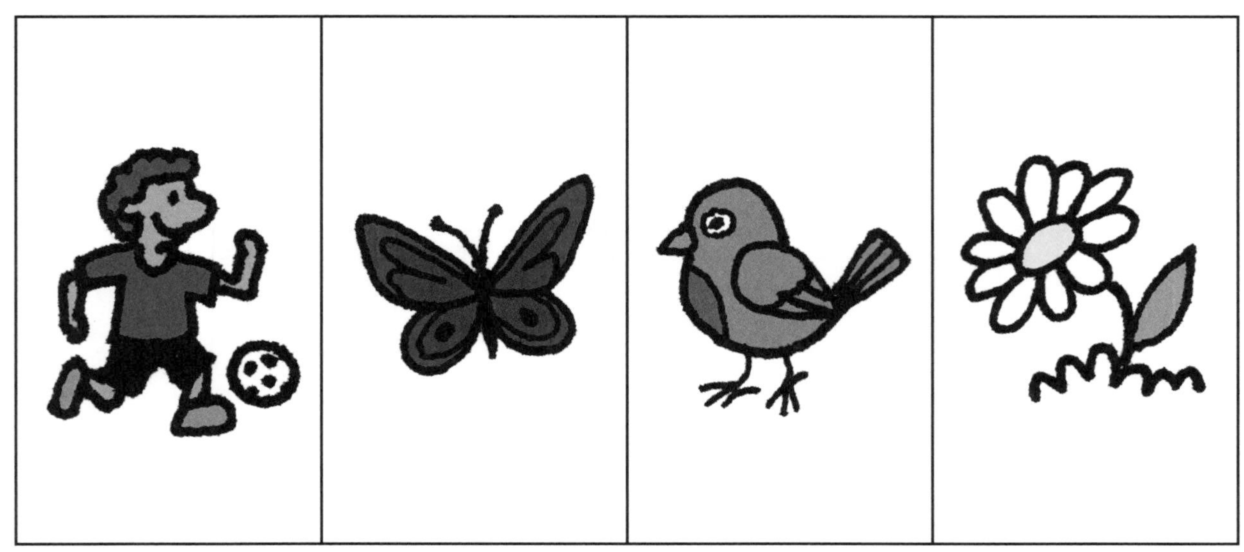

Walk through the toy shop

Maths focus: Use pictograms to represent data, read data from pictograms.

A game for two to four players.

What you need:

- Walk through the toy shop game board (p82).
- Walk through the toy shop pictogram base grid (p83).
- Walk through the toy shop toy cards (p84).
- Walk through the toy shop, What's your score? cards (p85).
- A 1–6 dice (CD-ROM).
- One counter per player.

Instructions: Game 1

1. Shuffle the What's your score? cards and place them face down.
2. Players start at the shop door and take turns to throw the dice, moving in any direction across the board to the checkout. They cannot move backwards.
3. If a player lands on a toy, they collect the matching Toy card and put it on their Walk through the toy shop pictogram base grid. If they land on a toy where all of the cards have been taken, they can choose a different Toy card.
4. When all players have reached the checkout, they turn over the top What's your score? card and work out their score, keeping count with counters.
5. If there is a tie, the player with the most toys in total wins.

Instructions: Game 2

Play as for Game 1.

1. If you land on a toy where all of the cards have been taken, miss a turn.
2. If you land on an empty cell, have another go.

Teacher notes

This is a game of chance so all players have an equal chance of winning. The pictograms produced provide a good opportunity to ask questions to test players' knowledge.

Walk through the toy shop

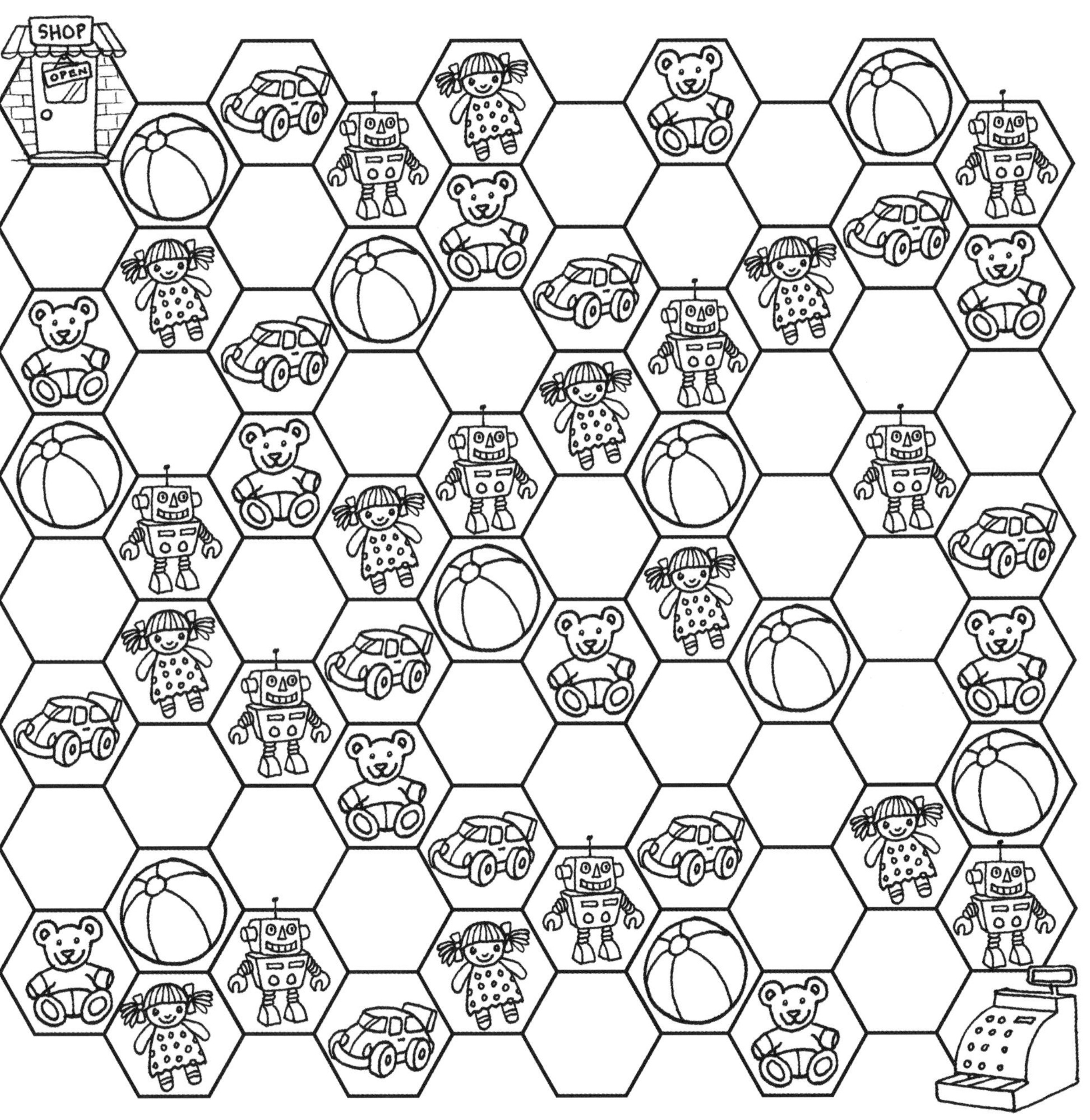

Walk through the toy shop pictogram base grid

Walk through the toy shop toy cards

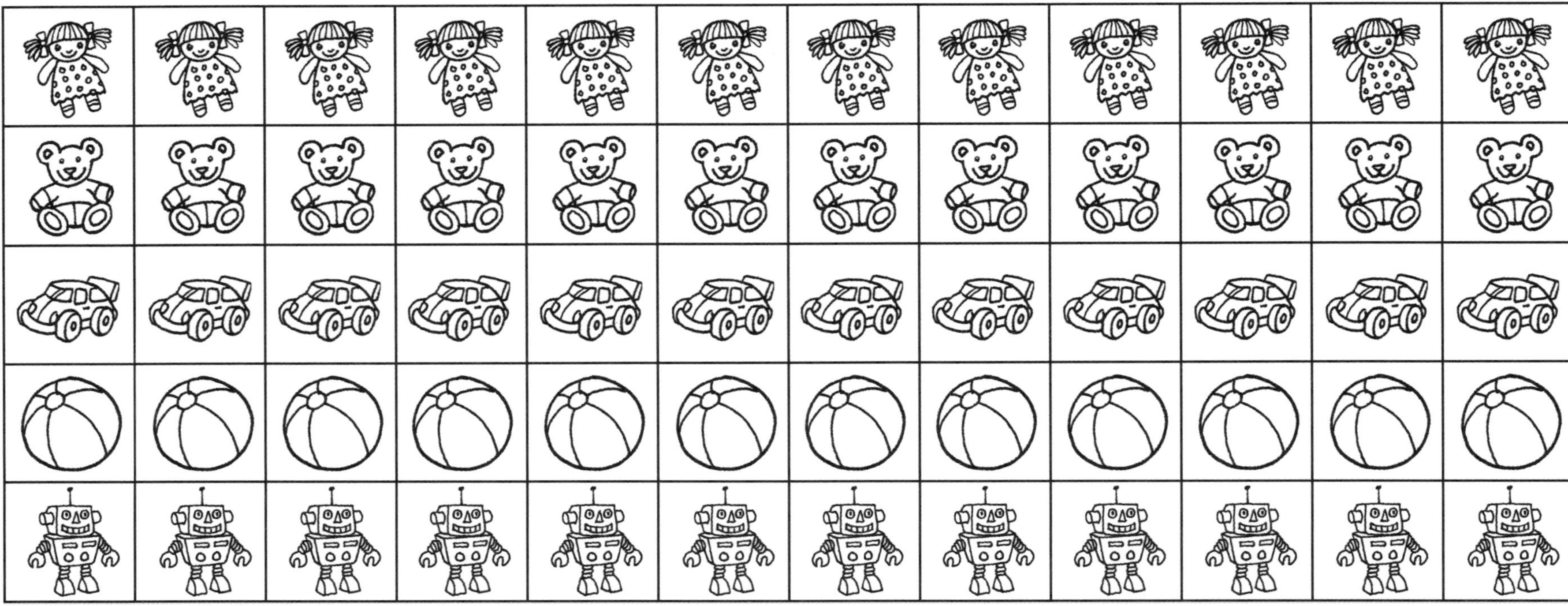

Walk through the toy shop, What's your score? cards

What's your score?

1. How many dolls do you have?
   The player with the most takes 1 counter.
2. How many teddies do you have?
   How many cars do you have?
   If you have more teddies than cars, take 1 counter.
3. How many robots do you have?
   How many balls do you have?
   If the difference is 2 or more, take 1 counter.
4. How many dolls do you have?
   How many teddies do you have?
   If the total is 10 or more, take 2 counters.

The player with the most counters wins.

What's your score?

1. How many cars do you have?
   The player with the most takes 1 counter.
2. How many dolls do you have?
   How many balls do you have?
   If you have more balls than dolls, take 1 counter.
3. How many robots do you have?
   How many teddies do you have?
   If the difference is 5 or more, take 2 counters.
4. How many cars do you have?
   How many teddies do you have?
   If the total is 4 or more, take 1 counter.

The player with the most counters wins.

What's your score?

1. How many robots do you have?
   The player with the most takes 1 counter.
2. How many teddies do you have?
   How many dolls do you have?
   If you have more teddies than dolls, take 1 counter.
3. How many dolls do you have?
   How many cars do you have?
   If the difference is 3 or more, take 1 counter.
4. How many balls do you have?
   How many teddies do you have?
   If the total is 7 or more, take 2 counters.

The player with the most counters wins.

What's your score?

1. How many balls do you have?
   The player with the most takes 1 counter.
2. How many robots do you have?
   How many cars do you have?
   If you have more robots than cars, take 1 counter.
3. How many teddies do you have?
   How many balls do you have?
   If the difference is 6 or more, take 2 counters.
4. How many dolls do you have?
   How many cars do you have?
   If the total is 3 or more, take 1 counter.

The player with the most counters wins.